Enjoy my green world...

VEGETRONIC

VEGETRONIC.

ALEXIS GAUTHIER

preface

When I started my cooking apprenticeship, I was told that I should know by heart every single classic dish that made up French gastronomy. I was told I should know my Sauce Choron from my Hollandaise, that I should know what a Bercy garnish adds to a fillet of sole, that I should be reverential to everything Escoffier had ever said and done.

So I learnt it, and without realising, I became just another recipe follower.

JUICES

Page 28

VEGETABLES

Page 72

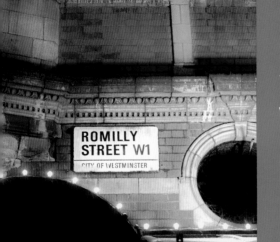

Since the industrial revolution, vegetables have been treated badly. They have been ignored, expelled, segregated, demoted and abused in every kitchen: top chefs, my mother, my sister, your wife, your son – everyone is guilty.

Vegetables are good for society but somehow society seems to prefer macho meat or feminine fish.

Vegetables are the ethnic minority of the kitchen – or maybe rather more like gay.

Yes.

Vegetables are gay.

Like gays, vegetables are half-accepted if they are happy to go along with the macho star of the dish.

Like gays, they are accepted as long as they significantly change their shape or consistency in order to sit alongside a girly fish.

They are slowly becoming more accepted, but they have not yet achieved the level of acceptance that they deserve.

Who wants to leave the exclusivity of vegetables to vegetarians?

NOT ME.

I believe that a vegetable can stand in the kitchen among the top ingredients.

A vegetable has the capacity to be the star of a dish: the central component where it can shine on its own.

Where its great flavour can stand alone or be married to fish or meat flavours, all the while retaining its own personality and being understood for what it is.

Well, I can tell you that vegetables have found a crusader in me.

I can carry the Green Cross and show the world from my kitchen (and this book) that salsify can match the finest fillet of beef, or pumpkin the most delicious Scottish scallops.

Equality for vegetables!

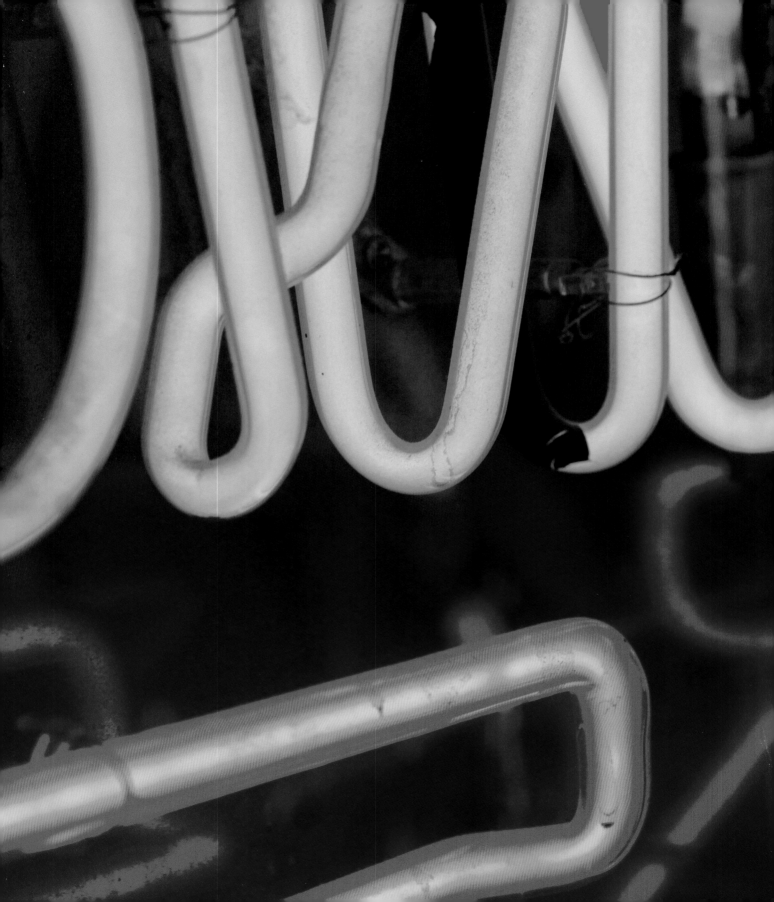

SYSTEM

To give you some guidance through the recipes in this book, I have separated them into three categories of difficulty:

EASY
A dish you can make quickly with little or no preparation, perfect for everyday situations.

MEDIUM
Intermediate skill level, a dish suited to special occasions, some preparation/technique required.

HARD
Restaurant level, more time and preparation required, sophisticated techniques/skills.

All recipes can be completed in a typically equipped kitchen. If special equipment is required, you will find sources on pages 374–375.

RECIPES BY D

1: EASY

2: MEDIUM

FFICULTY

3: HARD

CALORIES

I had been feeling slightly nauseous for a while. I would have a normal meal and then would feel a little bit dizzy. After spending a service at the pass in the kitchen, tasting the food before it was served to our guests, I would feel bloated, slightly weird and again a little nauseous.

I had a feeling of over-eating, even when I had just eaten a simple salad. It was strange, so I decided to pay a visit to my doctor. She didn't seem too worried by my symptoms and recommended a liver scan.

The first thing she asked me was: 'Do you drink a lot?' My answer was that I drank like an Englishman rather than a Frenchman – as I did not think that the few drinks I occasionally had would have an impact on my health.

So there I was, lying down in a doctor's room with my tummy covered in weird gel and looking slightly wary. The nurse came, rubbed a small camera over my stomach and the doctor took some pictures. It took five minutes, then I was asked to get dressed.

Seriously, I had been over-indulging on calories without realising. I started to think: ok, so every night I spoon in 30 bowls of risotto, have 25 slices of cooked meat, about 30 spoons of different meat and fish jus, eight to ten bread rolls, four or five different puddings, a tasting of puff pastries, Chantilly cream, mashed

'Counting calories was the only way to stay alive'

When I saw the specialist who had checked my scan, she was giggling and almost arrogant. 'Are you a chef?' she asked. 'Yes,' I replied, giving her a don't-you-know-who-I-am kind of look. With a very wide smile she said: 'You have a fatty liver. It is time to count. Count your intake of calories. You have been flooding your liver in fat and you are now paying the price for it. The only way out of this is to start counting calories and stick to what you are supposed to eat. No more, no less!'

I was a bit worried and wondered if this was going to be fatal. She looked at me as if I was stupid and said: 'A glass of wine is a glass of fat, so good luck.' She laughed, then asked me the name of my restaurant (which she had never heard of) and took £350 from my credit card.

potatoes, raviolis with different stuffings, sautéed vegetables, creamy mushrooms, spoons of consommé, creamy soup, browned buttered pieces of fish, glazed vegetables . . . every service, twice a day, six days a week for the last 15 years.

So I reckoned that I had been slowly poisoning myself, while making sure that my guests had perfectly cooked meat, precisely timed risotto, not over-sugared whipping cream, etc.

I hadn't even reached 40 years old and my liver was as fat as a French duck ready to be slaughtered. That reminded me I had been tasting our delicious Terrine de Foie Gras for the last 15 years at a rate of 15g per service, twice a day, six days a week, meaning that my body had tried to get rid of just over 150kg of foie gras.

That's about 300 fat duck livers!

Not exactly good for me.

Any anti-foie gras campaigner would have been delighted and would call it a fair revenge, unlike my gastroenterologist who now knew exactly the source of my illness!

Counting calories was the only way to stay alive. So how would I know how to calculate the number of calories I was consuming on a daily basis?

Easy! It took me 10 minutes of research on Google to find out what top athletes do as a rule of thumb to never exceed the right amount of calories.

First of all, I look at labels. By law in the UK, calories have to be published on

It is easy to use and is recommended by athletes. It is so easy to use that it takes less than 5 minutes per recipe to calculate. I enter the ingredients list with the quantity and the number of portions it is supposed to serve, and I press enter. My four-year-old daughter could work it out.

Then I made a small list of things that I know I should be careful with: a glass of wine, a slice of white or brown bread, a square of dark chocolate, a scoop of sorbet . . .

I did not start going to the gym three times a week, I did not stop drinking wine and I did not stop eating red meat. However, I have managed to lose 10% of my weight in the space of four months.

'I had the information and thought my customers had a right to know the calories in each dish'

supermarket packaging, so it is very easy for me to control my intake when I am at home and using pre-cooked food.

In the kitchen, I use an app called Caloriecount.com.

Now, almost two years down the line, I have not regained my old weight and at my last liver scan, the amount of fat covering my liver had been more than halved.

So when I decided to print calories on my menu back in Spring 2011, I did not do it out of trying to buy myself a good conscience. I had the information and thought that my customers had a right to know the number of calories in each dish. What if someone like me had entered my restaurant and needed to make sure of his or her calorie intake without compromising their choice?

There was nothing nannyish in trying to inform my guests. Just like the price of an item on the menu, I thought that it was fair to know the impact a particular dish may have on the body.

I did not change the way I cooked nor did I ever think of removing butter or cream from some recipes. Our Tasting Menu was 1900 calories.

A day's calorie intake!

JUICES

I like to season vegetables with juices. Not to bastardise their aroma and taste but rather to balance their flavour. Meat, fish, crustacean or vegetable jus: I find plenty of inspiration in those. They have become indispensable basic tools over the years for me to develop my recipes from. They feed my imagination and their combinations are never-ending.

I discovered this when I realised for the first time that I loved the taste of vegetables glazed in meat juice more than the meat itself. Sometimes I just felt like having the vegetables but not the meat that seemingly must come with it.

It is probably down to my mother or grandmother who would never wash a roasting dish before having used it a second time for roasting carrots, tomatoes and aubergines . . .

There would be aubergine and thyme the day after the leg of lamb, cardoon and bread after roast beef, carrots and salted butter after the loin of veal or braised endive after a baked sea bass.

But my favourite combination was probably the one my grandma would do a day or two after a roast chicken. She would have made sure to keep the roasting dish in the fridge, and then would stuff some tomatoes with herbs and soaked white bread. She would line the tomatoes in the roasting tray and cook them in the oven until the tomatoes had almost exploded! The taste of those tomatoes was unbelievable. They tasted like tomatoes but also had a meaty flavour to them because their flavours were enhanced by the juice and fat of the chicken. I could smell it and exactly break down the taste in the oven.

I knew it wasn't tomatoes and chicken cooking together but tomatoes cooked in chicken juice.

Here are the basic juices you will need to master if you want to start playing with taste and being creative.

CHICKEN JUS

For 500ml of ready-to-use jus

Difficulty level: easy
Calories: 100
Preparation time: 3 hours

300g chicken wings

50ml olive oil

½ onion (roughly chopped)

½ carrot (roughly chopped)

4 litres water

Cut the chicken wings into equal sizes. Pour a bit of olive oil into a large pan. When the oil is smoking, put in the chicken wings and roast them slowly at a low heat. When they are of the same colour (golden-brown) add the onion and carrot. Roast them well for about three minutes.

Then pour in 1 litre of water. Let the water reduce until it is almost dry in the pan, and then add another litre of water and reduce again. Repeat twice more until the juice is dark and the chicken wings have been completely cooked. Strain the jus. You can either keep it in the fridge for up to 4 days or you can freeze it.

When needed, just reheat it in a small pan with a teaspoon of butter.

LAMB JUS

For 500ml of ready-to-use jus

Difficulty level: easy
Calories: 100
Preparation time: 3 hours

300g not too fatty lamb trimmings (shoulder, neck or leg. Ask your butcher, they are usually free)

50ml vegetable oil (sunflower is usually best)

4 garlic cloves (crushed using the palm of your hand)

½ onion (roughly chopped)

½ carrot (roughly chopped)

4 litres water

Cut the lamb trimmings into equal sizes (4cm x 4cm is usually best). Pour a bit of vegetable oil into a large pan, and when the oil is smoking, add the lamb trimmings and roast them slowly at a low heat. Add the garlic cloves and stir without over-roasting. When the meat and garlic are of the same light brown colour, add the onion and carrot. Roast them as well for about three minutes.

Then pour in 1 litre of water. Let the water reduce until almost dry in the pan. Add another litre of water and reduce again. Repeat this once again until the juice is dark and the lamb trimmings are breaking down. Strain the jus. You can either keep it in the fridge for up to 4 days or you can freeze it. You will notice that this juice has quite a fatty consistency. Do not remove the fat as it holds all the flavour.

When needed, just reheat it in small pan with a teaspoon of butter before adding to your vegetables.

29

BEEF JUS

For 500ml of ready-to-use jus

Difficulty level: easy
Calories: 100
Preparation time: 3 hours

- 300g beef trimmings (not too fatty)
- 50ml olive oil
- ½ onion (roughly chopped)
- ½ carrot (roughly chopped)
- 20g unsalted butter
- 4 litres water

Cut the beef into equal pieces. Pour a bit of olive oil into a large pan. When the oil is smoking, put in the trimmings of beef and roast them slowly. When they are golden brown, add the onion and carrot. Roast them as well for about 3 minutes.

Remove the beef, carrot and onion and drain the pan. Return to the heat and add the butter. Make the butter foam until it almost turns brown (noisette) and add the beef, carrot and onion over then pour 1 litre of water. Let the water reduce until almost dry in the pan, and then add another litre of water and reduce again. Repeat this until the juice is dark and the beef trimmings are completely soft. Strain the jus. You can either keep this juice in the fridge for up to 4 days or you can freeze it.

When needed, just reheat it in a small pan with a teaspoon of butter before adding to your vegetables.

PRAWN JUS

For 500ml of ready-to-use jus

Difficulty level: easy
Calories: 100
Preparation time: 3 hour

- 50ml olive oil
- 200g prawn heads
- ¼ carrot (roughly chopped)
- 50g leek (white part thinly sliced)
- 2 soft tomatoes (roughly chopped)
- 1 teaspoon brown sugar
- ¼ lemon
- 10 basil leaves
- ½ bunch lemongrass
- 4 litres water

Into a large casserole dish, pour a little olive oil. When smoking, add the prawn heads and break them up with another pan or rolling pin. Just think of someone you hate and release your anger. Smash the heads, making sure that the brains have been emptied of their liquid.

Add the carrot, leek and tomatoes and roast for 3 to 4 minutes. Stir vigorously, and then add the brown sugar, lemon, basil and lemongrass.

Let everything roast for a couple of minutes then add 4 litres of water, to cover everything with liquid and cook at a slow simmer for about 2 hours. Then strain the juice and keep in the fridge or freezer.

Just like the meat jus, a prawn jus will need to be reheated with a small spoonful of butter before serving.

FISH JUS

For 500ml of ready-to-use jus

Difficulty level: easy
Calories: 100
Preparation time: 3 hours

- 40g butter
- 50g leeks (white part thinly sliced)
- ½ carrot (roughly chopped)
- 1 salmon head
- 100g fish trimmings
- 100g fish bones
- 1 teaspoon brown sugar
- ½ shallot (roughly chopped)
- 1 bunch thyme
- 2 soft tomatoes (roughly chopped)
- 2 tablespoons white wine vinegar
- 500ml cooking white wine
- 4 litres water

Into a large casserole dish, add the butter. When it starts foaming, add the leek and carrots and stir for 3 minutes. Then add the salmon head, fish trimmings and bones. Stir vigorously, and add the brown sugar, shallots, thyme, tomatoes and vinegar. Stir for another 2 minutes.

Add the white wine and reduce to almost dry.

Add the 4 litres of water and cook for 20 minutes at high heat. Strain and reduce for another hour.

There should be 500ml of fish jus by the end of this process.

Just like the meat jus or prawn jus, you will need to reheat the jus in a pan with a small quantity of butter before using.

BROTH

CHICKEN BROTH

Difficulty level: easy
Calories: 100
Preparation time: 3 hours

1 large chicken 1.6 to 2kg (ask your butcher for a boiler)

Neck, wings & chicken feet

3 litres water

4 large carrots (peeled)

3 turnips (peeled)

2 bunches celery (roughly chopped)

4 leeks (opened, sliced & washed)

2 garlic cloves

1 sprig thyme

1 bay leaf

Pinch table salt

1 teaspoon sea salt

1 teaspoon black peppercorns

Into a large cooking pot, put the chicken together with the neck, wings and feet. Cover with cold water and bring it to the boil.

When it starts boiling, remove from the heat, drain and rinse the chicken, neck, wings and feet. It is important to rinse the meat properly as it will make the broth very clear.

When the meat is well rinsed, put it back in the cooking pot together with the carrots, turnips, celery, leeks, garlic cloves, thyme, bay leaf and a pinch of salt.

Cover with cold water and bring to the boil. When it starts boiling, reduce the heat, making sure that it simmers very slowly.

Let the broth slowly cook for 4 hours. The broth may produce some grey froth, which is a mixture of blood remaining in the chicken and some dirt from the vegetables. You must remove this foam every hour or so.

Make sure to taste the broth after 4 hours. You may need to let the broth cook for another 1 or 2 hours. It happens when the chicken you are using is not of great taste. However if you are happy with the taste of the broth, remove it from the heat and add a teaspoon of sea salt and a teaspoon of black peppercorns. Let them infuse while the broth cools down.

Pass the broth through a muslin to remove all the impurities. Keep the stock in the freezer for up to 4 months or in the fridge for up to 4 days.

FISH BROTH

Difficulty level: easy
Calories: 100
Preparation time: 3 hours

1 salmon head

4 carrots (peeled & roughly chopped)

2 leeks (sliced & chopped)

2 bunches celery (roughly chopped)

3 shallots (peeled & chopped)

1 large onion (cut in 2)

1 garlic head (cut in 2)

1 litre dry white wine

3 litres water

1 teaspoon sea salt

1 teaspoon black peppercorns

200g fish bones (ask your fishmonger, they're usually free)

1 bay leaf

1 sprig thyme

4 cloves (planted in the onion)

Rinse the salmon head. Do not remove the eyes, as Escoffier would have taught me. Salmon eyes are delicious when they are cooked. Trust me.

Wash and rinse all the vegetables. Drain and dry them. Once again, it is very important that all vegetables are cleaned. They will help to make the broth as clear as possible.

Put a large cooking pot on the heat and pour in the wine, water, sea salt and black peppercorns. Bring it to the boil and add the remaining ingredients one by one.

Let the broth slowly cook for 2 hours.

Remove from the heat and let the broth cool down. Delicately remove the salmon head and remove the eyes. Eat them, they are delicious. Pass the broth through a muslin and let it cool.

You can either freeze it for up to 4 months or keep in the fridge for up to 4 days.

VEGETABLE BROTH

Difficulty level: easy
Calories: 100
Preparation time: 3 hours

6 carrots

4 turnips

2 leeks

2 bunches celery

½ bunch parsley

½ bunch chervil

2 litres water

½ teaspoon sea salt

½ teaspoon black peppercorns

Peel, wash and cut all the vegetables into chunky pieces. Make sure to wash and rinse the parsley and chervil as they may carry dirt. It is important that all vegetables are perfectly washed, to make the broth as clear as possible. Dry the vegetables on a clean cloth and place into a large cooking pot.

Cover with very cold water. The broth always needs to start cooking from very cold. You can even prepare the vegetables the day before and keep them in the fridge in the water they are going to cook in. Bring the pot to boiling point and add the parsley, sea salt, peppercorns and chervil. Let the broth cook very slowly for 2 hours.

Pass the broth through a clean muslin and throw away the vegetables. They will have lost all their taste to the broth so they are really redundant.

Taste the broth to see if it needs more salt or pepper. This is the last opportunity to rectify the seasoning of the broth by infusing a bit more sea salt or pepper while it cools down. It will keep in the fridge for up to 4 days or in the freezer for 4 months.

I love drinking this broth on its own but one of the great ways to appreciate it is to reheat it and break an egg into it. Leave to cook for 3 minutes and serve. It will be the best poached egg you will ever have.

FLOWERS

When I was young, I used to love deep-fried acacia, crêpes made with rose blossom water, a salad of in-flower dandelion and garlic flowers, and puddings made with mimosa.

My grandmother, Albertine, was a real genius with flowers. She used them everywhere: salads, stuffings, puddings and in a lot of her favourite wines and non-alcoholic drinks.

She never used a cookery book in her life, preferring to develop her own recipes. She loved gardening and eating. The two went hand in hand. She was right and her cooking became more and more floral over the years. She never tried to instruct me with her cooking. She never tried to convince me that she knew better than anyone else. Everything was natural for her and so long as it tasted good to her, it was fit to be served.

I thought that, as a typical Provençal grandmother, she would have found enough satisfaction from cooking fruits and vegetables. I was so wrong! She was the queen of flowers and herbs!

Studying my family history, I realised that we had a connection with North Africa and Italy: two places where they have been using flowers in cooking for generations. It must have been subconsciously in her genes!

In the northern region of Liguria in Italy, people have been using flowers as stuffing for meat, tarts and even fish for hundreds of years. Mixed with potatoes, for example, flowers bring a touch of seasonality. In Mexico, hibiscus or cactus are used in recipes dating back to the Aztec era.

& HERBS

In the Balkans, North Africa and the Middle East, flowers have been used for centuries, mainly for adding individual aromas to traditional recipes. Classic combinations like Ras el Hanout, herb-flavoured couscous, rose-petal marmalade, rose jelly or rose syrup in recipes are common there.

In South East Asia too, flowers have long been used. Pink lotus is served with rice wine in Laos and camellia leaves are served deep-fried or cooked like green vegetables in Indonesia. Japanese cooks use plum and peach flowers to make some fantastic and healthy infusions and to make delicious wine. Camellia is also a key ingredient in a celebratory meal for any person reaching the age of 90. Recipes using chrysanthemum leaves for steaming dumplings and stuffing crab or fish are also common throughout South-East Asia.

Easy to grow and easy to look after, flowers can be a great source of inspiration. Most flowers are edible. You can add a touch of exotic flavour with just a few edible plants grown in your garden or on your balcony.

DAYLILY RISO

Difficulty level: medium
Calories: 350
Preparation time: 40 minutes

Daylilies are easily grown and are attractive ornamental plants. They are also one of the tastiest plants in my garden. This plant can tolerate heavy clay and shady space. I particularly like the young leaves when they are not too fibrous. You can serve them in salad with a few drops of reduced Italian red wine (Vino Cotto), salt, pepper and olive oil. You can also dry the leaves to make a paste to use as a soup thickener.

Serves 4

- 2 cups daylily buds (blanched & chopped to an almost paste texture)
- 2 cups daylily foliage (quickly deep-fried in oil)
- 40g salted butter
- 40g shallots (peeled & finely chopped)
- 160g long-grain brown rice
- ½ teaspoon tamarind powder
- 20g freshly grated ginger
- 100ml dry white wine
- 2 litres water
- 300ml olive oil
- 160g baby squid (cleaned & thinly sliced)
- 1 lime juice
- Salt & pepper
- 40g flaked almonds

When the leaves are a little bit older, they can be pan-fried and served like spinach. You will be amazed by their salsify taste! They actually sometimes taste more like salsify than salsify. I recently heard some people argue that they taste like creamed onion.

Either way, it is a very special ingredient. The other good thing with this lily is that you can actually eat the root freshly grated in salad or rubbed against meat before cooking it. It tastes amazing!

Prepare the daylily buds and foliage.

In a large, thick-bottomed pan, melt a teaspoon of butter, then add the shallots. Stir until the shallots get hot and shiny.

Cook slowly for 2 minutes and add the rice. Stir continuously while making sure that neither the rice nor the shallots get coloured.

Add the daylily paste, tamarind powder and fresh ginger and stir. Add the white wine and allow it to bubble and reduce for 3 to 4 minutes. Then start adding the water ladle by ladle for 18 minutes while continuously stirring. Add 200ml of olive oil at the end and divide between 4 soup plates.

In a separate pan, quickly fry the baby squid in smoking oil until they start releasing water. Drain and put them back in the pan with a spoon of butter, the juice of one lime, salt, pepper and the flaked almonds.

Add the squid and almond on top of the rice. Add the foliage of a few deep-fried daylilies on top of each plate and serve.

CHRYSAN

THEMUM

On 1 November each year France celebrates the dead. Toussaint is a day of remembrance for families who have lost loved ones and also a day of joy and celebration for florists across the country.

It is a day when millions of over-priced chrysanthemums are brought to adorn tombs for the delight of . . . erm . . . well, no one really! I always wondered what the point was of spending a fortune on some really ugly plants that absolutely no one would ever thank you for.

So if you are heartless enough to think only about your own pleasure rather than that of the dead, you must transform these plants into something useful, hence the following recipe for burnt wine.

If you feel bad about it, you can always buy some dried chrysanthemum leaves from any good Asian food market.

FLOWER WINES

I have been living in the UK for many years now, but if there is something that I still admire it is the constant need to find a good excuse for alcohol consumption: celebrations, business meetings, friend gatherings, sport, end of the week, weekends . . . Anything is an excuse to indulge. Well, now I have just created another one: gardening. You will never come across as an obsessed alcoholic any more, but rather like a sophisticated gardener who can transform plants into alcohol. Brilliant.

CHRYSANTHEMUM BURNT WINE *(Pictured)*

Difficulty level: easy
Calories (per glass): 213
Preparation time: 2 hours 30 minutes

Serves 6

1 litre dry red wine

2 handfuls dry chrysanthemum leaves

2 oranges (peel)

1 bay leaf

½ cinnamon stick

½ vanilla pod

Boil the red wine for 5 minutes and add the dried chrysanthemum leaves. Boil for another 5 minutes and remove from the heat. Let the leaves infuse for 1 hour.

Pass the liquid through a clean muslin cloth and put back in a clean pan. Add the remaining ingredients and boil for 5 minutes.

Let it infuse for another hour.

Filter once again and reheat just before serving.

SAGE WINE

Difficulty level: easy
Calories (per glass): 229
Preparation time: 2 months

For 1 bottle

10 dried sage leaves

1 bunch dried thyme

1 tablespoon honey

1 bottle white wine

Chop the dried sage and thyme leaves and mix them with the honey. Add the white wine and mix until the leaves look mushy.

Let it macerate for 12 hours. In order to get the full taste of the sage, you will need to stir the maceration every hour.

Strain through a muslin cloth and bottle it.

Keep for 2 months before drinking.

FLOWER WINES

DANDELION WINE

Difficulty level: easy
Calories (per glass): 213
Preparation time: 2 months

Serves 4

2.5 litres water

4 handfuls dandelion flowers (or wild pissenlit) equivalent to 150g

4 handfuls dandelion flowers (or wild pissenlit) equivalent to 150g

1 teaspoon grated ginger

1 orange (peel)

1 lemon (peel)

1kg caster sugar

1 teaspoon dry yeast

150ml dry white wine

Boil the water and wait until it has cooled down (about ten minutes).

Clean the flowers after removing the stem. Cover them with the boiled water and let them macerate overnight.

Add the ginger and the orange and lemon peel, bring to boil and let them cook for 30 minutes. Filter through a muslin cloth and then add the sugar.

Add the dry yeast, with the wine. Cover the pan with a kitchen towel and put a lid over it. Let the wine ferment for 2 days at room temperature.

Leave the wine to rest in the bottle for at least 2 months before drinking.

ROSE WINE

Difficulty level: easy
Calories (per glass): 213
Preparation time: 1 month

Serves 6

200g dry rose petals

1 tablespoon honey

1 bottle dry white wine (e.g. a good value white Côtes du Rhône)

Before the end of summer, dry some rose petals, preferably from the most powerful plant. Mash the petals with honey and mix them with the wine.

Let the mixture macerate for 12 hours in a bowl covered with a cloth at room temperature. Filter through a muslin cloth. The rose wine may look a little cloudy at this stage but you should not worry as this will settle during the resting time.

Keep in the bottle for one month minimum and drink very cold.

This wine is perfect when drunk with roasted nuts or preserved fruits.

FUCHSIA

The fuchsia is a great little shrub for the shady part of your garden. It produces little flowers all through the summer and those are followed by tasty small fruits. Everyone at home loves these little fruits, especially my neighbour's cat who has been helping himself. One day the cat is going to pay for that! I just wonder what the cat might taste like – would his meat be very fuchsia-ish?

FUCHSIA-TOFU-GINGER MIX

Difficulty level: medium
Calories: 95
Preparation time: 30 minutes

Serves 4

100g fuchsia leaves

100g fuchsia fruits

2 tablespoons honey

2 tablespoons olive oil

2 tablespoons soy sauce

10g pickled ginger

300g hard tofu block

20g pink shallots

2 spring onions

Black pepper

1 tablespoon bonito flakes

This is the best way to eat the fuchsia (not the cat).

In a bowl, mix the leaves together with the fruits.

Add one spoonful of honey, one spoonful of olive oil and one spoonful of soy sauce. Add the chopped pickled ginger and keep at room temperature.

Slice the hard tofu block into ½cm-thick slices and line them on a serving tray. Chop the shallot and spring onion and sprinkle over the tofu. Add a bit of black pepper. Pour on the remaining honey, soy sauce and olive oil.

Pour the mix of fuchsia over it and add some flaked bonito before serving.

Serve cold.

LATE-SUMMER TOMATO & FUCHSIA SALAD

Difficulty level: easy
Calories: 80
Preparation time: 15 minutes

Serves 4

4 large Roma tomatoes (with a shiny dark-red colour)

2 garlic cloves (peeled & roughly chopped)

100g mix of fresh fuchsia leaves & flowers

150ml good-quality olive oil

Salt

Fat Italian tomatoes in summer paired with fuchsia are a perfect match. You must prepare them a little in advance and once they have both released their delicious juices, you will want to dip back into it again and again . . .

Clean the tomatoes and pat dry. Cut them into thick slices of about 1cm and put them in a large bowl. In a different bowl, crush the garlic with the fuchsia leaves. When the fuchsia-garlic mix reaches a paste consistency, add olive oil and salt. Pour the dressing on the top of the tomatoes and add the fuchsia flowers.

JASMINE-SCENTED HYDROMEL

Difficulty level: easy
Calories (per glass): 280
Preparation time: 10 minutes Fermentation time: 20 days Rest time: 2 months

This is a fermented honey wine drink which is as old as human civilisation. I've added jasmine and rose petals. When you drink it you feel as if the gods themselves have just entered the party and you can smell their perfume.

For 4–5 750ml bottles

3 litres water

300g honey

3 handfuls strongly scented dry rose petals

1 handful jasmine leaves

1 egg

250ml Muscat wine

Boil the water in a large pan and add half of the honey. Let it boil for 3 minutes, then add the rose petals, jasmine leaves and the egg. Stir for 3 minutes with a whisk, then remove from the heat. Let the stock infuse for 1 hour. Then cover it with a tea towel and leave it at room temperature for 20 days.

By this time, it will have fermented. Filter the stock through a clean muslin cloth and add the Muscat wine.

Store in tightly sealed bottles and leave to rest for a minimum of 2 months.

Note: You should always use untreated rose and jasmine petals, preferably from your garden. If you don't have one, make sure to buy your petals from a reputable shop.

LEMON BALM

My garden is full of lemon balm from the end of March until early July when the leaves become too large and less intensely flavoured. They have a slightly peppery, lemony taste to them. I love them in salads when teamed with lobster and crunchy vegetables. I also love lemon balm infusion: it tastes a bit like lemony spinach – strange yet very pleasing and a lot more interesting than mint infusion, for example.

LEMON BALM, PEAR & OYSTER

Difficulty level: hard
Calories: 60
Preparation time: 30 minutes

Serves 4

200ml dry white wine

500ml water

12 rock oysters (open & rinsed)

2 Williams pears (thinly sliced & kept in lemony water)

150g fresh lemon balm leaves (½ blanched & thinly chopped)

20g shallots (peeled & thinly sliced)

50ml whipping cream

Rock salt

Black pepper

In a pan, bring the white wine and water to the boil. Add the oysters and leave for 2 minutes. Refresh them in ice and keep them on a clean cloth to gently dry.

Place the slices of pear on a clean, flat surface. On each slice, spread a spoonful of thinly chopped lemon balm leaves, topped with a few thin slices of shallot. Place an oyster on each one.

Roll them up like small cannelloni and wrap a fresh lemon balm leaf around each one. Top each small cannelloni with a little whipping cream, rock salt and black pepper.

LEMON BALM INFUSION

Difficulty level: easy
Calories: 0
Preparation time: 5 minutes

Serves 1

Handful lemon balm

Hot water

Take a handful of freshly picked and washed leaves with a bit of stem still attached. Then pour some almost boiling water over and let it infuse for 5 minutes. Drink while still hot.

Lemon balm is so plentiful in my garden that I provide the restaurant with its annual stock for free.

LOVAGE BLOODY MARY

Difficulty level: easy
Calories: 140
Preparation time: 10 minutes

Lovage is very easy to grow in full sun or in a light shade position. I covered my side garden wall with lovage. It grew so much that it blocked the sun from the black tomato I was so proud of. After harvesting the leaves I will remove the plant from my garden – it is too invasive. Lovage has an interesting taste. When cooked, it is a bit like bitter celery. It is nice to add a few lovage leaves when preparing a green stuffing.

Serves 1

2 measures vodka

5 measures tomato juice

20g lovage leaves (quickly blasted in a food processor)

1 teaspoon lemon juice

4 dashes Worcestershire sauce

4 drops Tabasco sauce

Pinch celery salt

Pinch black pepper

Lovage's peppery flavour is always a nice addition. However, as it is such a powerful herb, I always suggest that it is used with caution. It can be extremely overpowering.

Try a Bloody Mary with the lovage juice and it will be the best you ever had.

Combine, shake and strain all of the ingredients.

Serve over ice.

Celery and tomato heaven.

LOVAGE & PEPPERMINT BUBBLEGUM

Difficulty level: hard
Calories: 20
Preparation time: 30 minutes

I have managed to crack the bubblegum mystery. As a child, I would dream of being able to make sweets to impress my friends. My proudest moment would have been to create BUBBLEGUM. Magical, the only sweet that could be shaped and would last for hours. Finally I have mastered the art of bubblegum making. I don't dream of synthetic flavour anymore. Now it's real peppermint for its freshness and lovage for its punch. A child's nightmare and an adult's heaven . . .

Serves 1

- ½ **bunch peppermint**
- 20 **lovage leaves**
- 20g **corn syrup**
- 1 **tablespoon gum base**
- 1 **teaspoon liquid chlorophyll**
- 20g **icing sugar**
- 30g **cornflour**

Blend the peppermint and lovage with the corn syrup until you get a very liquid syrup. It's ok if there are still a few bits inside. Place it in the fridge.

Make sure the gum base is at room temperature. Put it in a bowl and start softening it with the palm of your hand. When it starts to soften, put the bowl either in a microwave oven at full power for 30 seconds or in a conventional oven for 5 minutes at 180°C.

Add the peppermint syrup and the chlorophyll. Continue mixing the gum with your hand.

Add half of the icing sugar and continue pressing the gum with your hand.

On a clean surface, sprinkle some cornflour and continue pressing and folding the gum base in with the cornflour until it starts getting really soft.

Add the remaining icing sugar and continue flattening the gum.

When the gum is easy to flatten, cut some shapes and sprinkle them with cornflour so they don't stick together.

You can keep the gum for up to 2 weeks in a closed tupperware box.

MARSHMALLOW & RICOTTA RAVIOLI

Difficulty level: medium
Calories: 200
Preparation time: 45 minutes

This easily grown plant likes both dry and moist soil and requires a sunny position. The leaves are perfect for stuffing when mixed with ricotta. Everyone asks me where I found this amazing spinach. It is tender and soft, retaining its green colour like no other green leaves when cooked. Just perfect!

Serves 4

Stuffing

- 500g marshmallow leaves
- 200g chopped leeks
- 2 tablespoons ricotta cheese
- 2 eggs
- 20g grated Parmesan
- 50ml olive oil
- Salt & pepper

Pasta

- 200g flour
- 2 eggs
- 1 tablespoon water
- 1 teaspoon white wine vinegar
- Pinch salt

Making the stuffing

Wash and roughly chop the marshmallow leaves.

Wash and slice the leeks.

Heat a little olive oil in a pan. Add the chopped leeks, salt and water. Cover and cook for 3 minutes. Add the marshmallow leaves and cook for another 3 minutes. Drain and chop very finely.

Put the chopped ingredients in a big bowl then add the ricotta, eggs and pepper and mix together. Taste and season again. This stuffing should be very peppery (I like it like that). Add a bit of olive oil and grated Parmesan.

Making the pasta

You can either buy some ready made from Chinatown (delicious), or use the following recipe.

Mix everything in a bowl with your hands. Once you have a smooth even dough, cover with clingfilm and let it rest for at least 1 hour in the fridge.

Roll out the dough very thinly (good luck if you haven't got a pasta machine) and cut it into circles of 5cm x 5cm.

In each little circle of pasta, place one spoonful of stuffing and cover with another piece of pasta. Seal the borders by gently pressing on them.

Boil some water in a saucepan with a bit of salt. Throw in your stuffed pasta and wait until the pasta comes back to the surface of the boiling water. Wait another 30 seconds and remove them.

Serve on a plate with plenty of olive oil, grated Parmesan and black pepper. This recipe makes about 20 ravioli shapes.

MIMOSA

The fluffy little flowers in late winter and early spring are edible. They make great sweets when served at the end of the meal to accompany coffee or tea. They are also a perfect snack during the day, just deep-fried and tossed in icing sugar.

CRISPY MIMOSA FLOWER

Serves 4

Difficulty level: easy
Calories: 95
Preparation time: 15 minutes

300g mimosa flowers

100g caster sugar

50ml water

50ml vegetable oil

5g icing sugar

Dry the flowers for 3 weeks after harvesting.

In a pan, put the caster sugar together with the water. On a very high heat, bring it to a caramel-like colour, then remove the pan and throw in the mimosa, together with the vegetable oil.

Stir vigorously and remove from the pan, transferring onto an oiled tray. Let the flowers cool down, then roughly chop with a knife into small pieces when fully cooled. Sprinkle with icing sugar and serve.

CHOCOLATE & MIMOSA MOUSSE

Serves 4

Difficulty level: medium
Calories: 380
Preparation time: 40 minutes

200g dark chocolate (70% minimum)

175g whipping cream

1 handful dried mimosa flowers

2 teaspoons icing sugar

In a thick-bottomed pan, pour the dark chocolate and melt it at a very low heat. Make sure to stir the chocolate once melted to remove any thick pieces of chocolate.

In a bowl, whip the cream until it's on the verge of being stiff.

Once the chocolate has melted, slowly pour it into the cream and carry on whipping until the mix is blended well together. Fill 4 low tumbler glasses with the cream and store in the fridge for at least 20 minutes before serving.

Just before serving, sprinkle the dried mimosa flowers over the chocolate mousse.

Add a bit of icing sugar and serve.

CORSICAN MINT

Broccoli & cauliflower fake risotto

Difficulty level: easy
Calories: 140
Preparation time: 30 minutes

Corsican mint is a very delicate and low-growing plant, which likes a shady position in your garden. It is also the perfect mint for salad. You will notice that the taste is not too strong but will last a long time. The infusion made from it is very good for your health, especially when you have a cold.

Serves 4

- 200ml olive oil
- 40g shallots (finely chopped)
- 50ml dry white wine
- 200g broccoli heads (cut into small 1cm x 1cm cubes)
- 200g cauliflower (broken into small pieces)
- Salt
- 330ml water
- 20g mascarpone
- 40g grated Parmesan
- 50g freshly picked tiny Corsican mint leaves
- Pepper

In a large pan on low heat, pour 30ml of olive oil and stir in the shallots. Slowly cook for 3 minutes until the shallots look brilliant and soft. Add the white wine and reduce for 2 minutes.

Then add the broccoli, cauliflower and a pinch of salt. Stir gently, making sure you don't break the pieces of broccoli. Add the water and carry on stirring with a spoon for 3 minutes.

Add the mascarpone and stir until it has dissolved completely in the mix. Let it boil for 2 minutes and add the Parmesan and the remaining olive oil, making sure to constantly stir.

When the mix seems amalgamated, add the mint and pepper and serve quickly.

Everyone will think that you have made a very light broccoli and mint risotto, not realising that the rice texture is actually from the cauliflower!

ROSE-PETAL SORBET

Difficulty level: medium
Caloriess: 280
Preparation time: 4 hours

Rose petals are not very often used in traditional French cuisine. Too feminine, too delicate. Not an ingredient Escoffier would have ever dreamt of being associated with. I discovered so many fantastic ingredients the day I decided to move away from classical French training. Realising that rose petals were more than something that looked good in a bouquet was seriously life-changing!

Serves 4

- 380g sugar
- 530ml water
- 80g rose water
- ½ vanilla pod (cut in 2)
- Zest of 3 lemons
- 15g rose petals (untreated)
- 350ml Champagne
- 4 teaspoons pomegranate syrup
- 4 small packets space dust (optional)

In a heavy-bottomed saucepan, bring to a boil the sugar, water, rose water, vanilla pod and lemon zest.

Add the rose petals and let them infuse.

Pass through a muslin cloth and chill.

Add the Champagne and churn in an ice cream machine.

Serve in a bowl, drizzle pomegranate syrup over and sprinkle on some space dust just before serving.

VIOLET

Early May is the best time to remove the leaves from the stems. Dry them out for 2 weeks. This will leave you enough time to decide what to do with them. Violet is such fantastic little flower. It can really be a chef's best partner. It is so versatile and can be used in syrups, essences, jellies, creams or cakes.

VIOLET & FENNEL SOUP

Difficulty level: easy
Calories: 120
Preparation time: 45 minutes

Serves 4

50ml olive oil

3 large fennel bulbs, thinly sliced

1 jacket potato (peeled & roughly chopped)

Pinch Fleur de sel (or smoked salt if you can find some)

1.5 litres water

2 handfuls violet leaves (quite fresh if possible)

Pepper

Into a large pan, pour a splash of olive oil. When the oil is smoking, put in the sliced fennel and the potato together.

Stir and add the salt. Add some water and 1 handful of violet leaves. Cover and allow to cook slowly.

After half an hour, pass through a mixer and add the last handful of violets.

Serve when hot with a pinch of cracked black pepper.

VIOLET GRANITÉ

Difficulty level: medium
Calories: 110
Preparation time: 3 hours

Serves 4

2 litres water

400g sugar

2 handfuls dry violet leaves

In a pan, pour the water and the sugar. When boiling, add the violet leaves, remove from the heat and let them infuse until it has cooled down.

Place the mixture in a bowl and put in the freezer.

Every 2 hours, take it out and scratch it with a fork so it turns into the texture of a granité.

Serve in frozen glasses topped with some fresh petals.

VIOLET JELLY

Difficulty level: medium
Calories: 188
Preparation time: 2 hours

This recipe reminds me of my grandmother who used to feed me jelly for breakfast on toasted bread with salted butter. She had a great collection of jellies! The flavour she gave me would depend on the weather, her mood or simply what was left in the cupboard, but my favourite was her violet jelly.

Serves 10

1kg Golden Delicious apples

50ml water

1kg caster sugar

½ lemon (juice)

200g dried violet leaves

Peel the apples and rinse them with hot water. Put them in a large pan and cover with water. When boiling, remove from the pan (they should be soft by then) and break them into pieces.

Into a large pan, put the sugar and the water. Cook on a low heat and when the sugar is almost turning brown, add the broken apples and stir for 15 minutes on a very low heat. Add the lemon juice and the violet flowers, remove from the heat and leave to cool.

When the jelly has cooled down, stir again and pour into jars.

I love it when there are a lot of chunky pieces of apples left in the jelly.

The taste of the violet becomes so strong within the apples that it is as if they had slept together!

OR, HOW DO YOU USE VEGETABLES AS A NATURAL DIVERSIFIER?

Sensibility plays a big role when it comes to treating a vegetable. The more responsive you are, the more you are likely to find that a vegetable is the perfect tool to express yourself via cooking.

Firstly, open your eyes and look at where you are. Where do you stand? What time of the year is it? What do you want? What does your body need? Have you ever wondered what surrounds you, and if there is anything that has a parallel life to yours?

Be aware of your senses and use the seasons as a guideline, this will naturally bring natural diversity. Everything will start feeling so normal. Yet so inspiring!

You'll surprise yourself by getting excited to be able to buy the first asparagus in May. It will remind you that winter is now gone for good and spring has already started to show its fantastic produce.

You'll be sad to be using those delicious summer squashes for the last time this year, but will be happy to know that the pumpkins are already showing great promise for the coming autumn.

That is the amazing life of vegetables and you must live at their pace. Not too fast or too slow.

They go on and on following the months. By giving you a sense of time, they also make you feel part of the season.

They make you feel part of it all.

They make you feel alive!

VEGET

ABLES

Vegetables, dry or fresh, are an immense source of inspiration for me. I actually think that they are the bases of my 'alimentation': I think of them as a starter, main course or even pudding.

They are very often sidelined by chefs and recipe books. They are in danger of becoming the exclusive property of vegetarians. And I don't want that. Vegetables are for all of us.

We tend to think that vegetables are just there to be good for you. We have been told that we should eat spinach on a regular basis in order to get enough iron, folic acid and potassium. And by the way it also regulates my blood pressure, boost my immune system and has anti-cancer properties. So let's order a side dish of spinach. It doesn't matter if it tastes good or not. It's good for me. So, should I care if it tastes good?

Yes, of course you should care. There are so many ways to cook them: boiled, grilled, roasted, simmered, braised . . .

There are so many ways to season them: salt, pepper, meat juices, fish juices, vinegar reduction . . .

I actually think that you can be a lot more creative with vegetables than with meat or fish. You can play with their textures, their shape and their smell in ways impossible with meat or fish. And if you use vegetables as they come into season, you will naturally change your diet and bring more excitement to your meals.

That is the amazing life of vegetables. They follow the months giving a sense of time passing. They also make you feel alive. Yes, you are alive!

ASPARAGUS

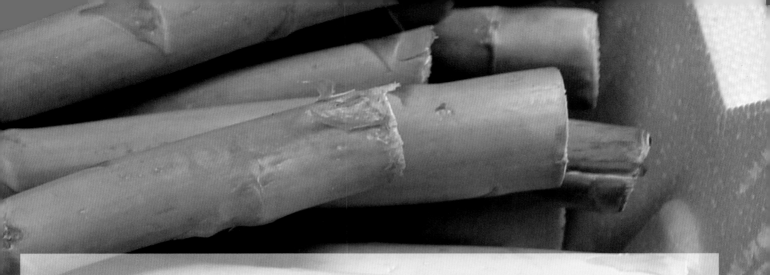

Whether green, white, purple or wild, the asparagus has been popular for centuries.

The Ancient Greeks thought that they were aphrodisiacs and Louis XIV of France wanted to have asparagus on his table every day from December. The first unsustainable king; his family paid for it later!

We know now that asparagus is rich in potassium, folic acid, vitamins C and K . . . And I know from my grandmother that they are also good for the kidneys.

The season begins in March and finishes in June. You should not be tempted to eat asparagus before or after. White, green or purple, asparagus has to be very fresh if you want to eat it at its best (usually 2 days after it has been harvested).

To make sure that you are buying the right asparagus, it has to be slightly wet at its base and it has to be firm yet easy to break. A soft asparagus is an asparagus that has lost its taste, but we knew that already – not only with asparagus.

The best way to cook asparagus is to pan-fry it in order to stabilise its chlorophyll. By using this technique, it will always end up looking green and shiny and, most importantly, will not turn dark and will never taste boiled and washed out.

GREEN ASPARAGUS

Confit lemon, poached quails' eggs & Parmesan crisps

Difficulty level: hard
Calories: 224
Preparation time: 1 hour

Serves 4

Asparagus
1 bunch green asparagus

Salted water

Poached quails' eggs
50ml water

2 tablespoons white wine vinegar

Salt

12 quail's eggs

Lemon confit
2 lemons

20g white sugar

2 tablespoons white wine vinegar

Parmesan crisps
100g finely grated Parmesan cheese

1 teaspoon flour

Sauce
100ml balsamic vinegar

100ml red wine

10g unsalted butter

For the asparagus

Remove the hardest part at its base, about a fifth of the asparagus, depending on its freshness. The fresher the asparagus, the longer the softer part will be. Peel the asparagus halfway, removing the little spikes, and boil them for 5 minutes in salted water. As soon as they are cooked, place in cold water and drain once cold.

For the poached quails' eggs

Boil the water with the white wine vinegar and salt. Break the eggs into boiling water for 2 minutes then place them in cold water.

Making the lemon confit

Peel the lemons. Slice the peel into equal strips. Melt the sugar and white wine vinegar in a pan. Add the juice and skins of the two lemons. Cook at a very low heat until the strips of lemon look opaque and the liquid has evaporated.

Making the Parmesan crisps

Mix the Parmesan together with the flour and pass it through a sieve, making sure that only the finest particles are kept. Into a non-stick pan, on a low heat, sprinkle the mix, making round shapes. Remove once they have melted without letting them colour.

Making the sauce

Into a small pan, add all the ingredients. At low heat, reduce until the liquid has evaporated by half.

Serving the dish

Reheat the asparagus in a pan with a little bit of butter, salt and pepper. Place the confit lemon and asparagus on the plate. Add the quails' eggs and Parmesan crisps. Pour the sauce around and over.

WARM SALAD OF GREEN ASPARAGUS
Gnocchi of ricotta & crunchy bacon

Difficulty level: hard
Calories: 250
Preparation time: 1 hour

Serves 4

Asparagus
- 200g green asparagus
- 8 slices streaky bacon (chopped)

Dressing
- 100ml port
- 1 teaspoon brown sugar
- 100ml olive oil
- 2 tablespoons white wine vinegar
- 10g unsalted butter

Gnocchi of ricotta
- 125g ricotta cheese
- ½ tablespoon flour
- 1 tablespoon grated Parmesan
- 1 egg
- Salt & pepper

Serving
- ½ glass water
- 20g butter
- 2 tablespoons grated Parmesan
- Pepper

For the asparagus

Remove the hardest part at its base, about a fifth of the asparagus, depending on its freshness. Remove every little spike around it. Slice lengthways very thinly (2mm) with a Japanese mandolin (or a very sharp knife if you haven't got one) and keep in icy water so the slices become crunchy and slightly bent.

Grill the bacon at 220°C. Alternatively, you can pan-fry the bacon until it turns golden.

Making the dressing

In a pan, pour the port, together with the brown sugar, olive oil and white wine vinegar. Reduce to half of its original volume and add the butter.

The reduction will turn thick once the butter has been absorbed by the liquid. Remove from the heat and keep at room temperature until serving.

Making the gnocchi of ricotta

Mix all the ingredients in a food processor until it turns into a smooth paste. Rectify the seasoning with salt and pepper and put in the freezer for 20 minutes.

Once the ricotta mix is cold, form some small quenelles with two coffee spoons and poach them in boiling water for 3 minutes. Remove from the water and keep them covered in clingfilm until serving.

Serving the dish

Reheat the gnocchi in a pan with half a glass of water, 20g of butter and 2 tablespoons of Parmesan.

Meanwhile, in a vegetable bowl, toss the asparagus with half of the dressing. Add salt and pepper. Place the gnocchi on the plate and cover them with the asparagus. Add the bacon and pour the remains of the dressing around it.

Add some cracked pepper and serve.

MEDLEY OF WHITE ASPARAGUS
Garlic leaves & crispy chicken skin

Difficulty level: medium
Calories: 125
Preparation time: 45 minutes

When I think of a vegetable as the 'star' of a dish I need to balance its entire composition. White asparagus, despite its refinements, needs a lot of help. As a general rule: add crunch if soft, add sweet if bitter, add green if white, add animal if vegetable.

Serves 4

Asparagus
500g (1 bunch) white asparagus

100g wild garlic leaves

Chicken skins
100g chicken skin (your butcher will usually give it away for free)

40g butter

Salt & pepper

Serving
50g unsalted butter

20g ground almonds

10 tablespoons chicken jus

For the asparagus

Cut off the hardest part of the asparagus.

Peel from top to bottom, making sure not to remove too much of the flesh. Cook the asparagus for 4 minutes in boiling salted water and rinse under cold running water.

Wrap two garlic leaves around the bottom of each asparagus spear.

For the chicken skins

Flatten the chicken skins out on a clean surface and score them slightly with a knife without cutting them too much. Season them with butter, salt and pepper.

Sandwich them between two baking trays and cook in the oven at 180°C for 10 minutes.

Serving the dish

Just before serving, heat the butter in a large pan. When it starts turning brown, add the asparagus and toss until they starts to turn golden. The leaves at their base should start to become a little crispy. Add the ground almonds and place the asparagus on a plate.

Reheat the chicken jus and pour it around the asparagus.

Add the crispy chicken skins on top of the asparagus.

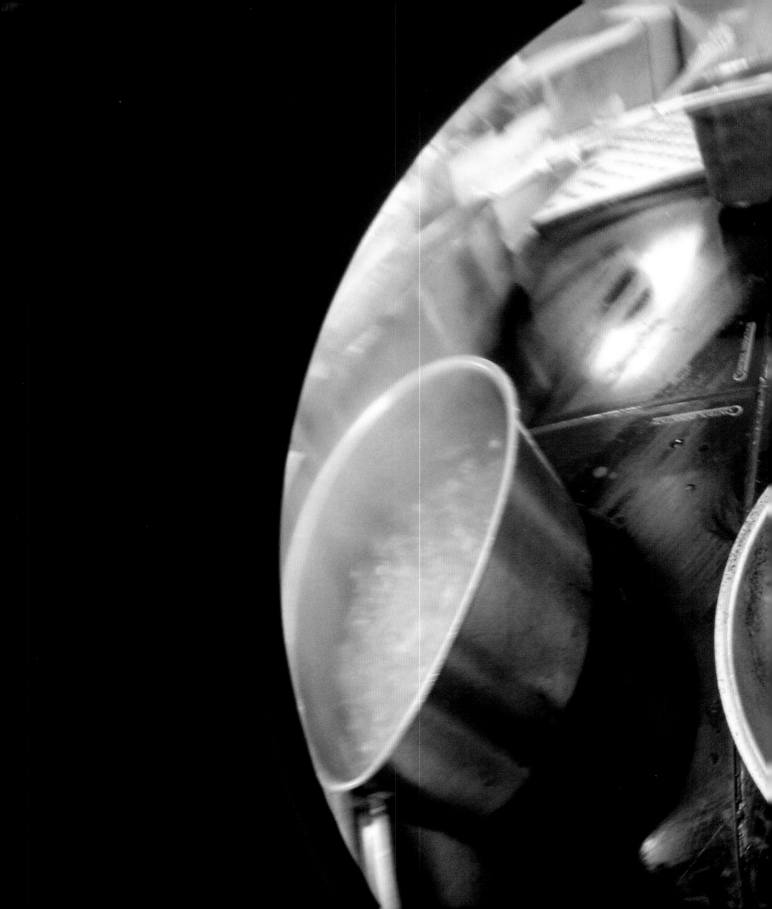

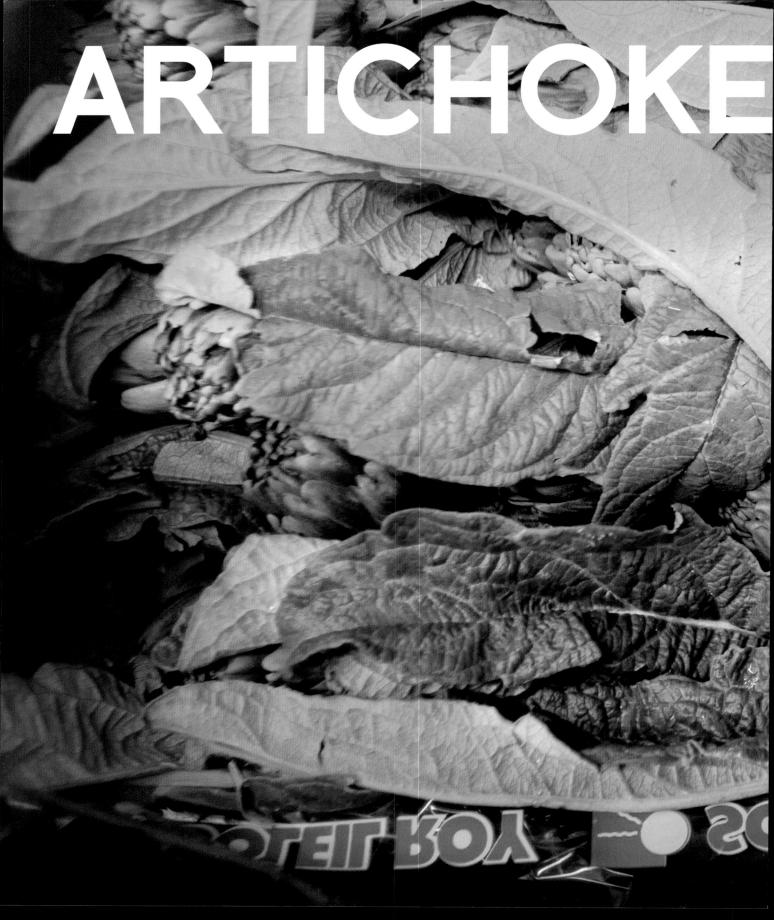

ARTICHOKE

ARTICHOKE 'BARIGOULE'

Difficulty level: hard
Calories: 150
Preparation time: 45 minutes

This dish was my worst nightmare as a child. It looked ugly, tasted weird and its texture was so off-putting that I would probably have preferred eating haggis, just so you can feel my disgust. I just couldn't understand how my parents would find any pleasure in having this dish other than enjoying seeing me suffer. I guess getting old is a bit weird: you tend to enjoy things that you would have detested in your youth – so alongside hairy chests and Thatcher's rhetoric, Artichoke 'Barigoule' is something that I now really like.

Serves 4

1 shallot

1 carrot

8 button mushrooms

40g smoked streaky bacon

16 small purple artichokes

2 tablespoons olive oil

2 sage leaves

1 glass white wine

8 large slices Parma ham

1 tablespoon unsalted butter

2 glasses chicken broth

Salt & pepper

Cut the shallot, carrot, mushrooms and streaky bacon into small cubes.

Remove the outside leaves of the artichokes. Go around them with a very sharp knife to get rid of any green skin that is left.

Remove the hairy inside of the artichokes and put the artichokes in very cold water.

Pour a bit of olive oil into a hot pan. When it starts smoking, add the carrots, shallots and salt.

Stir while making sure not to give it any colouration. When the carrots and shallots are shiny, add the mushrooms and bacon. Continue stirring for an extra minute and add the sage leaves and half a glass of white wine.

Let the liquid evaporate, and strain.

Stuff each artichoke with the chopped mix of vegetables and wrap them in half a slice of Parma ham.

Place the artichokes in a sauté pan and add the butter, chicken broth and the remainder of the white wine.

Cover and cook for 20 minutes. Serve on a large plate with a pinch of pepper.

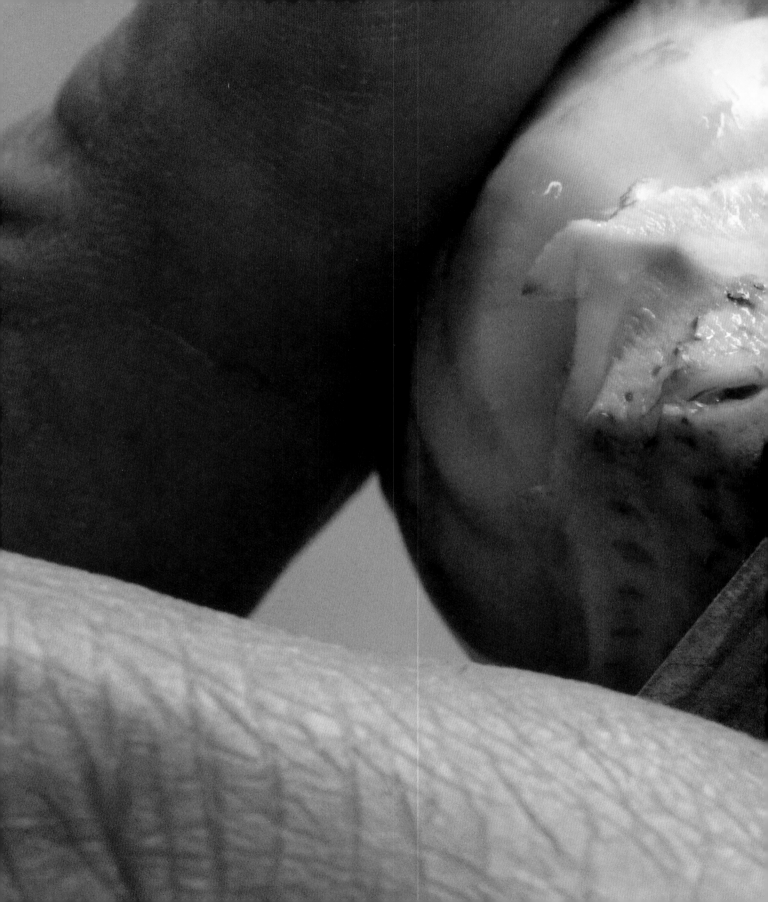

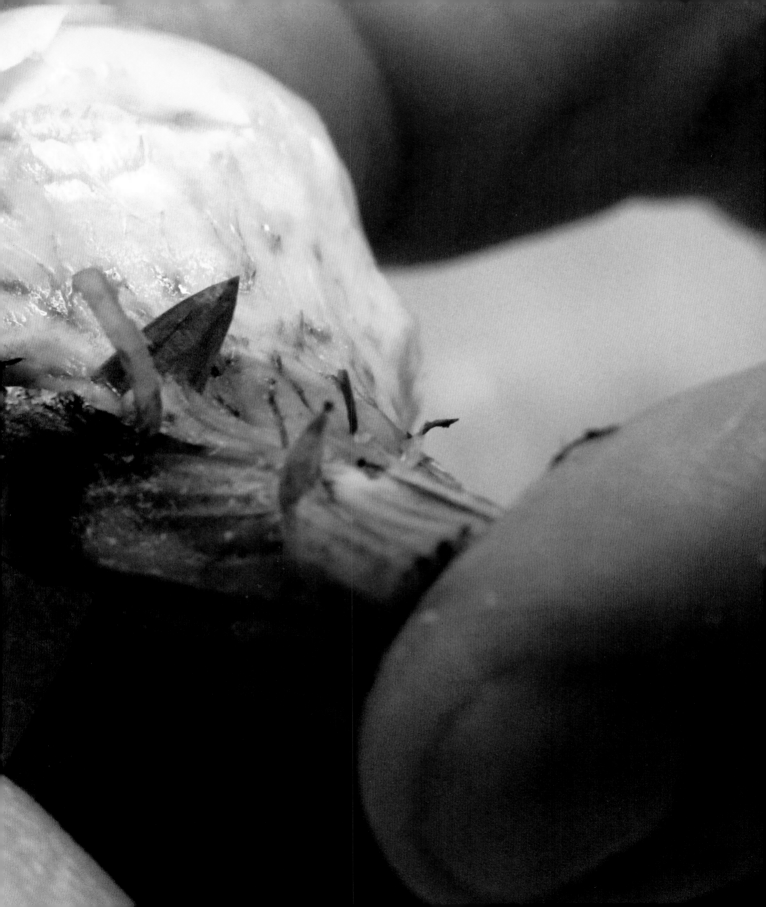

JERUSALEM ARTICHOKE & CHERVIL SOUP

Difficulty level: medium
Calories: 220
Preparation time: 30 minutes

The Jerusalem artichoke is one of the easiest vegetables to cook and also one of the tastiest. A winter or spring vegetable, it is of the same family as potatoes but its taste is as delicate as an artichoke. Very rich in phosphorous and potassium, very filling as well: 100g of Jerusalem artichokes equals 80 calories! The good thing with this vegetable is that you can't perform miracles with it. I mean you cannot transform its shape, for example. You cannot transform its taste or its texture. It is a simple and real vegetable and I love it like that.

Serves 4

- 1kg Jerusalem artichokes
- 30g butter
- Salt & pepper
- 300ml low-fat milk
- 1 bunch chervil
- 100ml water

The Jerusalem artichoke never had the same success as the potato or the artichoke and even now is still struggling to get stocked in supermarkets. I have always wondered why.

Peel and chop the Jerusalem artichokes and keep them in icy-cold water.

Place the butter in a hot pan. When it turns brown, add the Jerusalem artichokes and sauté with salt.

As soon as they are slightly coloured, add the milk and cover with a tight lid. Cook at low heat for 6 minutes.

After that, pour the contents of the pan into a blender and mix until you have a uniform and beige liquid cream.

Clean the food blender and blend the bunch of chervil, reserving a few leaves for decoration, with the water, salt and pepper.

Reheat the Jerusalem artichoke soup and serve in hot soup cups or Bordeaux glasses. Pour the chervil mixture over the soup and serve with more chervil leaves on top.

JERUSALEM ARTICHOKE & CRISPY CHICKEN SKIN

Difficulty level: hard
Calories: 288
Preparation time: 1 hour

Is there a better dressed vegetable dish than this one? A mushy vegetable that is the real star of a dish. If it was on its own, it would be dead boring. The moment you add a little bit of texture (crispiness from the chicken), a depth of flavour (brown butter and Parmesan) and the deliciousness of slightly fat meat jus it is not naked any more. With the help of a few accessories it shines and takes on another dimension.

Serves 4

- 100g chicken skin (your butcher will usually give it away for free)
- Salt & pepper
- 320g Jerusalem artichokes
- 100ml olive oil
- 20g unsalted butter
- 70g grated Parmesan
- 100ml chicken jus

On a clean surface, flatten the chicken skins and season them with salt and pepper. In a very hot non-stick pan, fry each piece until it turns crisp. It takes usually 4 minutes frying on each side of the skin to turns crisp. Rest on a grill. When cold and hard, cut into triangle shapes.

Peel the Jerusalem artichokes and make sure that you don't leave any skin on. Put in cold water until you cook them to retain their bright white colour.

In a large pan pour a bit of olive oil and drain the artichokes properly before putting them in the hot pan. Add half of the butter to the pan and wait until it turns brown. Add the Jerusalem artichokes and roast them slowly on a low heat, then add salt and put a lid on. Check very often. The artichokes should release enough water during the cooking process that transforms into steam so they won't burn.

Check the Jerusalem artichokes often because there is a point after 4 minutes when they are cooked and are still in their original shape. At this moment, bring the heat very high to evaporate any water left in the pan.

Add the remaining butter and make it turn brown. Shake the pan, making sure not to smash the artichokes.

When it has browned, sprinkle over the grated Parmesan and remove from the heat.

Serve on 4 small plates and place the triangles of chicken skin over the artichokes.

Reheat a little chicken jus in a pan and pour onto each plate.

GRILLED AUBERGINE

Shaved bonito, almond, sultanas, yogurt & shallots

Difficulty level: medium
Calories: 115
Preparation time: 45 minutes

Aubergine is often described as bland. The real purpose of aubergine is to act as a vehicle for other flavours while giving a very particular texture. I can't think of a similar texture that would come close to that of a cooked aubergine. I have found two particular cooking techniques which really enhance the beauty of an aubergine: grilling and baking.

Serves 4

- 2 large aubergines
- 1 head iceberg lettuce
- 100ml olive oil
- 2 tablespoons balsamic vinegar
- Salt & pepper
- 60g Activia yogurt
- 1 shallot (peeled & thinly chopped)
- 40g flaked almonds (slightly coloured under the grill)
- 40g sultanas
- 2 tablespoons bonito flakes

Wash the aubergines and cut them into ½cm-thick slices. Grill each slice dry (without any oil) on both sides and rest on a kitchen cloth. The aubergine should be soft but not dry or crisp.

Cut the iceberg lettuce into 1cm-thick slices. Line them on a tray and pour over the olive oil and balsamic vinegar. Make sure the lettuce is well covered. Add some salt and pepper and leave to soak for 10 minutes. The lettuce should absorb the oil and vinegar while retaining its crunchiness.

Meanwhile, pour the yogurt into a vegetable bowl and mix in the chopped shallot. Add some salt and pepper to taste.

Put the sliced lettuce on a plate and cover it with the cold grilled aubergine. Then cover with the yogurt and shallot mix. Sprinkle over the almonds and sultanas and finish by adding the bonito flakes.

Bonito is used in this recipe: dried fish flakes which tremendously enhance the original flavours they are associated with. Sainsbury's stock it sometimes, alternatively you can buy it from Amazon.

AUBERGINE TOASTS

Difficulty level: easy
Calories: 235
Preparation time: 1 hour

Serves 4

4 tablespoons olive oil

2 large aubergines (cut into 1cm cubes)

Salt & pepper

1 shallot (chopped very thinly)

1 garlic clove (chopped very thinly)

2 tablespoons red wine vinegar

100ml chicken jus

1 baguette

Preheat the oven to 180°C.

In a large sauté pan, pour some olive oil. When the oil starts smoking, add the aubergines with a pinch of salt and start to sauté them. Make sure not to give any colouration just yet and wait until the aubergine starts releasing its water. As soon as it happens, drain the aubergine in a colander. Arrange the aubergine in a shallow roasting tray and cook in the oven for 8 minutes.

When ready, cool them down and mix in a bowl with the shallots, garlic, 2 tablespoons of vinegar and the olive oil. Mix well so the aubergine has the texture of a coarse mash. Taste for salt and pepper and add the chicken jus. Keep in the fridge until serving.

Set the oven to grill position. Cut some slices of bread (1cm thick), brush some olive oil on both sides and grill them on both sides.

When the bread is golden-brown, serve it on a plate accompanied with the cold aubergine purée.

BEETROOT FANTASIA

Crunchy apple, fresh goats' cheese & thyme

Difficulty level: hard
Calories: 180
Preparation time: 1 hour

Back at school, it seemed to me that every time I was having lunch there I was served beetroot salad as a starter. It was always heavily dressed and the mustard was far too powerful for the delicate taste of the beetroot. And on top of that I was always dead conscious of not having my tongue and teeth entirely red. Now beetroot is very much à la mode. There isn't a trendy restaurant in London that doesn't celebrate the pseudo-new life of this forgotten (at least for them) vegetable.

Serves 4

50ml olive oil

2 bunches fresh beetroot (peeled with 2cm stem attached)

Rock salt

2 litres water

25ml balsamic vinegar

120g fresh goats' cheese

Black pepper

4 small bunches fresh thyme

2 Royal Gala apples (thinly sliced)

Beetroot is now served in every way and in every form. Raw, half-cooked, honey-glazed, grilled, as a pudding, and I have even seen it featured as a pizza topping! (I have tried it and I can assure you that it tastes as it reads: disgusting.)

Beetroot is not an easy vegetable to marry. It has such a sweet and powerful flavour that you usually need something acidic and oily to go with it and balance its rich flavour.

Pour 20ml of olive oil into a hot pan. Once the oil is smoking, add the beetroot and sauté them until they get very shiny and slightly coloured. Add some salt and 1 litre of water. Cover with a lid and cook at a slow simmer for at least 15 minutes. Make sure to check that the water has not totally evaporated after 10 minutes. You may need to add another 250ml of water depending on how tight the lid is on the pan. Check how cooked the beetroot is by planting a small knife into the biggest beetroot. If it goes in and out without resistance, it means the beetroot is cooked.

Add the olive oil and balsamic vinegar to the betroot jus in the pan. Stir and let the beetroot jus, olive oil and balsamic vinegar come together and form a split dressing. Remove from the heat and let it cool.

In a vegetable bowl, break up the fresh goats' cheese with a fork. Add a tablespoon of olive oil, some salt, black pepper and fresh thyme. Serve the beetroot warm with a spoonful of goats' cheese.

Add the slices of raw apple and serve.

UPSIDE-DOWN BORSCHT

Difficulty level: hard
Calories: 264
Preparation time: 3 hours

Serves 4

Soup

50ml oil

10 chicken wings (cut in 2)

140g beef (bourguignon cut)

Salt

1 bunch dry fennel

½ bunch fresh marjoram

½ white onion (diced)

100ml red wine

1 litre chicken broth (see page 32)

3 raw beetroot (grated)

Garnish

40g butter

2 leeks (cleaned & shredded)

1 stalk celery (thinly sliced)

1 medium onion (peeled & diced)

6 Savoy cabbage leaves (boiled &
cut into small triangles)

200g beetroot (you can use vacuum
pack pre-cooked beetroot cut into
small cubes)

40g sour cream

Making the soup

In a sauté pan with a little oil, pan-fry the chicken wings with the pieces of beef, making sure that they turn golden-brown but are not burnt.

Add a pinch of salt, the dry fennel, marjoram, onion and the red wine. Reduce until the mixture is almost dry. Add the chicken broth and the grated beetroot. Cook at very low heat for 2 hours.

Remove the beef from the broth and thinly slice it. Divide it into 4 and place the slices at the bottom of soup plates.

Making the garnish

In a sauté pan, melt the butter and add the leeks, celery and onion. Slowly heat them while stirring with a spoon. Add the Savoy cabbage (keeping a little for a garnish), beetroot, salt and pepper. Constantly stir while the vegetables slowly continue to heat together. Taste and rectify the seasoning if needed.

Spoon the vegetables on top of the slices of beef in the plates and serve the beetroot and chicken broth on top.

Serve with sour cream on the side and garnish with some Savoy cabbage.

COLD SUMMER CREAM OF BROCCOLI & GINGER

Difficulty level: easy
Calories: 85
Preparation time (including chilling): 3 hours 30 minutes

Broccoli is a great way to start the day. You can drink the juice of broccoli. Clean it and put the heads in your juicer. I think that when it is mixed with fresh orange pulp, it is the perfect juice: not too sweet, not too bitter and with more than just the orange bits!

Or you can try this simple recipe.

Serves 4

1 large broccoli head (about 300g)

20ml olive oil

40g onion (peeled & chopped)

1 garlic clove (crushed)

Salt

40g ginger root (peeled & grated)

500ml water

Lime (zest)

Clean the broccoli under cold running water. Into a big pot, pour some olive oil. When it starts to smoke, add the broccoli and the onion and garlic.

Add salt and grated ginger root. Stir (making sure that nothing gets coloured) and add 500ml water. Cover and wait ten minutes.

Make sure that the broccoli is cooked, then put everything in a mixer.

You may have to add a little water to get the perfect consistency.

Keep in the fridge for a minimum of 3 hours before serving.

Don't forget to serve with a big splash of olive oil on the top of each glass and add some freshly grated lime zest.

WHOLE BROCCOLI

Grain mustard & crunchy radishes

Difficulty level: medium
Calories: 110
Preparation time: 30 minutes

Broccoli is one of the most nutritious vegetables! Good for its anti-cancer value and antioxidants, it is antiviral, full of calcium and vitamins. The problem is that in terms of cooking it doesn't leave much room for your imagination. You can't play with its shape and you can't really play with the way you cook it! During the '80s chefs thought that broccoli, because of its shape, would look good in the presentation of dishes. It was the '80s equivalent of micro-leaves! It was everywhere and it looked awful.

Serves 4

1 head broccoli

50ml olive oil

10g grain mustard

1 egg yolk

1 tablespoon balsamic vinegar

½ bunch long radishes (thinly sliced & kept on ice)

20g black radishes (thinly sliced & kept on ice)

Salt & pepper

100ml chicken jus

It is very rare to find broccoli as the main part of a dish in a restaurant or cookery book. But, as with many '80s things, it is meant to make a comeback very soon so let's set the trend and put broccoli as a centrepiece back on the menu.

Choose broccoli when its dark green colour is turning purple.

Wash under running water and dry it with a kitchen towel. Cut off the stem at the base of the head.

In a large pan heat some olive oil, add the broccoli and pan-fry it without colouring it. Then add a little water and cover for 5 minutes. When the broccoli is almost cooked (you will know when you can insert a knife without resistance), let the water left in the pan evaporate.

Prepare the dressing by whisking the grain mustard, egg yolk, the remaining olive oil and balsamic vinegar together until the mixture thickens a little.

Lay all of the radishes at the bottom of the plate. Place the broccoli head over them and cover with the dressing.

Pour over the hot chicken jus and serve whole at the table.

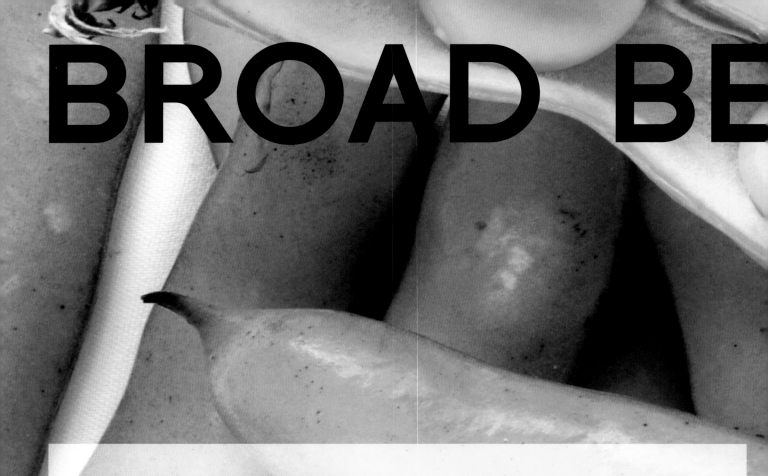

BROAD BE

This is one of the most delicate of all the vegetables I use. The best time to eat broad beans is when they are very young – pale green and very tender.

There is something not very exciting about the broad bean though. It takes an hour to peel two handfuls and just 3 minutes to eat them! Lucky are the ones who indulge on broad beans. They surely don't have to double peel them!

We can find broad beans from May to early September. Sadly, the late season bean is not as sweet and tender as the early one.

You can still prepare some superb cold broad bean soups when they become too astringent to be eaten raw.

These are 3 recipes to utilise the broad bean: the first one is for the early season, when they are small, sweet and pale green; 2 are for the end of the season, when they are too big, but still delicious when cooked.

AN

BROAD BEAN

BROAD BEAN & CHERVIL SALAD ON TOAST

Serves 4

Difficulty level: easy
Calories: 277
Preparation time: 30 minutes

1kg broad beans (double peeled)

½ cucumber

8 small round radishes

60g tinned tuna

2 tablespoons mayonnaise

1 lemon (juice)

½ bunch chervil (chopped)

½ bunch flat-leaf parsley

150ml olive oil

Salt & pepper

50ml aged balsamic vinegar

4 slices Pain de Campagne (rubbed with garlic, oiled & toasted)

8 anchovy fillets

Remove the beans from their shells (or ask someone to do it for you!).

Boil some water in a big pan. Throw the beans into it for 5 seconds then drain. Refresh under cold water, put them on a kitchen cloth and remove their thin skin.

Peel and slice the cucumber with a Japanese mandolin. Wash and slice the radishes, also with the mandolin.

In a large bowl, mix the tinned tuna with the mayonnaise and the lemon juice. Gently mix with a fork and taste. Add the chopped chervil and parsley and add a bit of olive oil. Taste for salt and pepper.

Put the broad beans in a bowl with the sliced radishes and cucumber. Combine the balsamic vinegar, salt, ground pepper and olive oil and drizzle over.

Cut each slice of bread into 3 long slices. Top each of them with the tuna mix. Then add the broad bean mix.

Add some anchovy fillets, olive oil, salt and pepper, and serve.

INFUSION OF BROAD BEANS WITH LEMON BALM

Serves 4

Difficulty level: easy
Calories: 120
Preparation time: 1 hour 30 minutes

3 litres water

½ carrot

½ onion

½ leek

1kg broad beans (unpeeled)

1 bunch lemon balm

Salt & pepper

50ml olive oil

This recipe should be used late in the broad bean season when the beans are very hard and flourished.

Into a big pot, pour the cold water with the carrot, onion, leek, unpeeled broad beans and half the bunch of lemon balm. Add a bit of salt and cook for 1 hour.

Add the remainder of the lemon balm and allow to infuse. Remove the lemon balm and serve the broth hot with the stewed vegetables.

Add a splash of olive oil just before serving and some cracked black pepper.

CHILLED SOUP OF LATE BROAD BEANS *Watercress & poached egg*

Difficulty level: medium
Calories: 260
Preparation time: 45 minutes

Serves 4

1kg broad beans (thickly chopped in their pods, about 1cm thick)

Salt & pepper

1 litre chicken broth

White wine vinegar

4 eggs

½ bunch curly parsley

In a large pan, heat some olive oil. When the oil is smoking, throw the chopped broad beans and stir vigorously in order to stabilise the chlorophyll in the beans without giving any colouration.

When the broad beans are very green and shiny, add some salt and the chicken broth and put a lid on.

Cook for 7 minutes on a high heat. The broad beans should be still green after 5 minutes and should melt in your mouth.

Remove everything from the pan. Blitz in a food processor and pass through a large-holed colander.

Put it in the fridge overnight (minimum) and serve the following day. The flavour of broad beans tends to intensify when you leave the soup to rest for at least 12 hours before serving.

Boil some water in a deep pan. Add the vinegar. Break the eggs one by one into the boiling water and cook them for three minutes. Remove them from the water and refrigerate.

Quickly pan-fry the parsley in a little sunflower oil,

Place a cold poached egg in the middle of each bowl and top with the crispy parsley. Pour the cold soup around and serve.

WHITE BEAN SOUP

Peppered, with crunchy lettuce, flat-leaf parsley, red wine & garlic bread

Difficulty level: medium
Calories: 158
Preparation time: 2 hours

The white bean is usually a summer vegetable. It can also be purchased dry and cooked throughout the year. I like the texture of the white bean: I like it when puréed and when mixed with olive oil, herbs and salt. It becomes like a light mayonnaise. It is also so good for you: it removes excess cholesterol, cleans your digestive tract and is rich in protein.

Serves 4

- **100g dry white beans (borlotti, cannellini or coco)**
- **2 litres water**
- **½ onion**
- **1 carrot**
- **½ leek**
- **1 bay leaf**
- **Salt & pepper**
- **2 slices Pain de Campagne**
- **2 garlic cloves**
- **1 Cos lettuce**
- **1 large bunch flat-leaf parsley (roughly chopped)**
- **200ml very dry red wine**

Place the white beans in a large pot and cover with water. Bring to the boil then drain.

Run the beans under cold water and put them back in the pan. Cover with water and add the onion, carrot, leek and bay leaf. Yes, you only need one bay leaf. Cook the beans very slowly and make sure that there is plenty of water in order for the beans to 'swim' in water. The beans tend to double in size while cooking!

You know the beans are cooked when they just melt with a little bit of pressure between your teeth. When you reach this point of cooking you'll realise that we have not put any salt in this preparation. The salt would have broken their thin skin during cooking.

Remove the pan from the heat and add a pinch of sea salt and allow it to infuse in the beans while they cool in the liquid.

Taste again and add more salt if you feel like it. Always salt with sea salt otherwise when you over salt this dish you won't be able to rectify the mistake. The best salt to use is Fleur de Sel de Guérande or de Camargue but the price is far too expensive for this dish.

Blend the beans with their cooking stock and slowly reheat them.

Meanwhile, toast the Pain de Campagne and rub the garlic cloves against them. Cut into chunky cubes.

Wash the lettuce and separate the crunchy leaves from the stalk.

Serve in large soup bowls. Place the parsley in the middle of the bowl, top with the bean soup, then the crunchy leaves and the Pain de Campagne. Pour a bit of red wine over each plate and add some black pepper.

HOT SUMMER WHITE COCO BEAN SOUP

Difficulty level: medium
Calories: 245
Preparation time: 2 hours

Having grown up in Provence, I used to eat a lot of cold food during the hot summers of my childhood. Refreshing melon, cold aubergine stews and salads of sweet and bright tomatoes. There was however an exception in our summer food. I would really look forward to having this hot soup served to me in summer. It was served burning hot and I remember being so impatient to eat it that I would burn my tongue at the first spoonful. The hot combination of white bean, basil, Parmesan and thyme is still vivid in my mind. No other food reminds me more of my summers in Avignon.

Serves 4

300g white coco beans

½ leek (white part only, roughly chopped)

1 carrot (roughly chopped)

1 onion (roughly chopped)

1 bay leaf

2 garlic cloves (thinly sliced)

10 sprigs dry thyme

1 bunch basil

2.5 litres water

1 courgette (roughly chopped)

1 over-ripe tomato (chopped into cubes)

8 spring onions (thickly chopped)

1 tablespoon sea salt

100g rigatoni pasta (cooked, refreshed & chopped)

1 tablespoon soy sauce

80g grated Parmesan

Rinse the dried coco beans under cold water for 1 minute. Put them in a large cooking pot with the leek, carrot, onion, bay leaf, garlic, thyme and half of the basil bunch. Cover with water and cook slowly for 15 minutes.

Add the courgette, tomato and spring onions. Cook for another 10 minutes.

Remove from the stove and add sea salt. Gently stir in the salt while making sure not to mush the ingredients.

Let the pot cool.

When you are ready to serve, reheat the beans to boiling point and add the pasta to the pot together with the soy sauce.

Serve in a hot soup plate with grated Parmesan and the rest of the basil leaves, chopped.

CABBAGE

The cabbage is not to everyone's taste, but there are so many varieties that if you look closely, you'll find one that appeals to you.

My fear had always been eating in a Chinese restaurant and having to smell boiled cabbage for the entire meal. There is something off-putting about it, but when I started to look beyond its smell, I found cabbage to be a very versatile and complex vegetable.

The cabbage is a winter vegetable and is considered a perfect food when it comes to healthy eating. Eaten raw, it detoxifies the stomach and colon. It improves digestion, stimulates the immune system, kills bacteria and is an antioxidant.

CARAMELISED SAVOY CABBAGE *Liver wrap*

Difficulty level: medium
Calories: 186
Preparation time: 45 minutes

Always buy Savoy cabbage when the leaves are very green. Perfect as a wrap or just roasted in brown butter with lard. When it comes to choosing a Savoy cabbage, make sure that you buy the heaviest and that its leaves are very tight.

Serves 4

- 1 Savoy cabbage
- 1 Cos lettuce
- 40g butter
- 5 garlic cloves (peeled & finely chopped)
- 40g onion (peeled & finely chopped)
- Salt
- 50ml olive oil
- 120g chicken livers
- 50ml Xeres vinegar
- 40g foie gras
- Soy sauce

Remove all of the dirty leaves from the cabbage. Cut the base and pull off all the greenest leaves. Put the leaves one on the top of another on your chopping board and cut them into thick slices of similar size.

Prepare the Cos lettuce by removing the leaves from the stalk, wash and keep them in the fridge.

In a large pot, put some butter on a low heat. When the butter starts foaming, put in the garlic and onion and cook them until they turn slightly brown. Add the shredded cabbage, salt and water. Cover and cook for 40 minutes.

Put some olive oil in a sauté pan. When the oil starts smoking, add the chicken livers and sauté them for 3 minutes. Add a teaspoon of butter and let it turn brown. Deglaze the pan with a dash of Xeres vinegar and stir. Remove from the pan and let the livers cool down a little.

Chop the foie gras roughly and place on top of the lettuce leaves. Add the cooked cabbage and chicken livers and serve with a dash of soy sauce.

RED CABBAGE

Always buy red cabbage when it is dark red, turning light purple. Do not go for the one which has its leaves starting to turn black or if the leaves seem too thin.

SALAD OF RED CABBAGE, GREEN DANDELION & CHICKEN JUS DRESSING

Difficulty level: easy
Calories: 75
Preparation time: 1 hour 30 minutes

Serves 4

- ½ red cabbage
- 2 bunches bitter green dandelions
- ½ bunch flat-leaf parsley
- 4 tablespoons olive oil
- 2 tablepoons balsamic vinegar
- Salt & pepper
- 4 tablespoons chicken jus

Cut the red cabbage thinly and rinse under cold water.

Put the shredded red cabbage in a bowl filled with ice and water and let it become crunchier for 10 minutes in the fridge.

Meanwhile, wash the dandelion leaves and parsley.

Put the olive oil, balsamic vinegar, salt and pepper into a bowl. Add the drained red cabbage, green dandelion and parsley. Mix and put on plates.

Add a bit of chicken jus to each plate and serve with black pepper.

BRAISED RED CABBAGE, CINNAMON, RED WINE & PORK BELLY

Difficulty level: medium
Calories: 330
Preparation time: 1 hour 45 minutes

Serves 4

- 1 whole red cabbage
- 160g pork belly
- 1 tablespoon sea salt
- ½ onion
- 1 Golden Delicious apple (peeled & chopped)
- 2 tablespoons cinnamon
- 2 tablespoons brown sugar
- 50ml cooking red wine
- 1 tablespoon goose fat (or 40g unsalted butter)
- Salt & pepper

Preheat your oven to 170°C.

Cut the red cabbage thinly and rinse it under cold water. Put it in the fridge for 10 minutes to make it crunchier.

Fill a pot with cold water and add the pork belly and a tablespoon of sea salt. Bring to the boil, drain and rinse the pork belly under cold water. Cut the belly into small cubes of 1cm x 1cm.

In a deep pan, put the onion, red cabbage, pork belly, apple, cinnamon, brown sugar, red wine, goose fat, salt and pepper. Stir, cover and cook in the oven for 1 hour.

Serve straight from the oven.

BRUSSELS SPROUT LEAVES

Bacon, chestnuts & chicken livers

Difficulty level: medium
Calories: 170-
Preparation time: 45 minutes

The first time I told my grandfather that I had decided to move to London to work he said: 'Why are you going there? It is where people eat Brussels sprouts! You can't make anything good with Brussels sprouts.' What he was referring to was a common belief in France that the British only eat grey-boiled Brussels sprouts at every meal to complement two kinds of potatoes. The French still believe that only they know what is good and how it can be cooked. The barbaric one is always the other one.

Serves 4

400g Brussels sprouts

100ml olive oil

50g carrot (diced)

50g white onion (diced)

4 slices streaky bacon (thinly sliced)

Salt

80g vacuum-packed chestnuts

40g unsalted butter

120g chicken livers

50ml white wine vinegar

200ml beef jus

I fell in love with Brussels sprouts the minute Mark Birley, the famous founder of Annabel's and Mark's Club, gave me this recipe. It was a classic garnish that his clubs used to serve during the sprout season and I can assure you that I am now a firm believer that the sprout is a very classy vegetable!

After washing them under cold running water, take one sprout at a time and remove as many outer leaves as you can, making sure to retain only the bright green ones. Any stained or yellowed leaves should be disposed of.

Despite their size, a good Brussels sprout always has tough, very green leaves. The leaves usually require 10 minutes of cooking in salted boiling water to tenderise them.

Once they have boiled, refresh them under cold water.

In a small pan, heat the olive oil until almost smoking and add the carrot, onion and bacon. Lower the heat and stir, making sure not to give any colouration. After a couple of minutes the carrots and onion will start looking more and more shiny. Add the Brussels sprout leaves and stir for another minute. Add some salt then the chestnuts. Cover and cook at medium heat for 5 minutes.

In small pan, heat the butter until it turns brown. Add the chicken livers and sauté them at high heat. Add salt and cook them for a further 2 minutes making sure to always shake the pan. Add the white wine vinegar and cook for another 30 seconds. Remove the pan from the heat and place the contents of the pan on a plate.

Reheat the beef jus and serve the Brussels sprouts leaves in soup plates topped with the chestnuts, chicken livers and the beef jus.

CARDOON

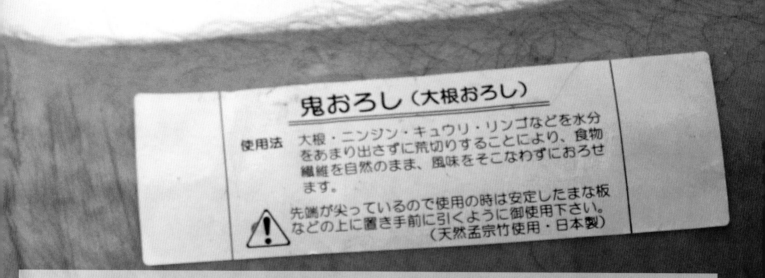

This vegetable was famously used by the Greeks and the Romans. It was grown widely at that time and was regarded as a real delicacy.

The cardoon is now something of a second-class vegetable, especially on this side of Europe. I was surprised to find that most of my customers didn't know it.

My mother, for example, used to make a gratin of cardoon for Christmas. She used to cook the cardoon with veal marrow, butter and olive oil. It was very tender and obviously dead rich!

In traditional French gastronomy, according to Escoffier, cardoons should be cooked in boiling salted water with a lemon cut in half. I don't have to tell you that this is absolutely the wrong way to eat cardoons and it was a shock to me to find out that nobody wondered if there was any other way to enjoy them.

Until I worked in Ducasse's kitchen. I discovered while there that it could be cooked to a 3-Michelin-star standard.

The way we cooked them was almost the same way as my mother did, except that we took a lot more care than she did to peel the cardoons. You have to use the sharpest knife in the kitchen. The cardoon is made of thin fibres that are almost invisible. So if you are not careful, you may think that every layer of skin has been removed, but as soon as it is cooked, the unpeeled layers of skin will turn black.

I can tell you that I had hours of bollocking and psychological bullying while at Ducasse. The head chef would find it very exciting to stand next to me as my cardoons were cooking. The moment one turned black, he would just destroy me in front of all of my colleagues, and repeat again and again that I should quit being a chef and turn to hairdressing instead!

I hated him.

My love for cardoons, however, has never diminished.

CARDOON

MELTING CARDOON GRATIN WITH PARMESAN

Difficulty level: medium
Calories: 230
Preparation time: 1 hour

Serves 4

- 1 cardoon head
- 50ml olive oil
- 80g butter
- Salt & pepper
- 750ml water
- 100ml beef jus
- 60g grated Parmesan

First, peel the cardoons and keep them in cold water. Into a large pan, pour a bit of olive oil and when hot, fry the cardoons, making sure not to colour them. Add the butter together with salt and pepper. Then add some water and cover.

Cook on a very low heat and simmer. Every 3 to 4 minutes, try to put a knife through the cardoon. When there is no resistance, remove the pan from the heat and let it cool.

Put the cardoons in a gratin dish and cover them with their reduced cooking stock, the beef jus and some freshly grated Parmesan. Put in a very hot oven (220°C) for 3 to 5 minutes.

Serve with a lot of pepper.

RAW CARDOONS WITH ANCHOVY SAUCE

Difficulty level: easy
Calories: 95
Preparation time: 30 minutes

Serves 6

- 1 cardoon head
- 40 small anchovy fillets
- 4 garlic cloves
- 2 boiled eggs
- Salt & pepper
- 2 tablespoons red wine vinegar
- 300ml olive oil

Peel the cardoons and put them in very cold water. Store in the fridge for 20 minutes and then drain.

With a pestle and mortar, mix together the anchovy fillets, the garlic, boiled eggs and salt and pepper until you get a thick paste. Add the red wine vinegar and olive oil. Taste and rectify the salt (depending on how salted the anchovies are).

Serve the anchovy paste in a bowl with the crunchy cardoons on the side.

CARROT

This is the most consumed root vegetable in the world. In a traditional French kitchen, the carrot is used almost everywhere. It brings sweetness to sauce and broth, adds texture to cream and velouté, and, most importantly, shines on its own when it carries a dish.

Carrot is the real star in the vegetable world.

CARROT

HONEYED CARROTS WITH TIGER PRAWNS & CUMIN

Difficulty level: medium
Calories: 150
Preparation time: 45 minutes

Serves 4

200g carrots

40g leeks (white part only)

50ml olive oil

2 tablespoons honey

1 teaspoon cumin

Salt & pepper

4 tiger prawns (peeled, head on, opened in 2)

20g butter

50ml prawn jus

Slice the carrots and the leeks (the same size).

Into a pan, pour some olive oil. When the oil starts to smoke, toss the carrots and leeks together. When the carrots and the leeks are starting to shine, pour in enough water to cover them. Add a bit of honey and cumin and cover with a lid for 2 minutes. Then remove the lid and let the water evaporate.

The carrots should be perfectly cooked when the water has totally evaporated. The carrots should be just tender. Taste and check if you need more salt, and add pepper.

In a very hot pan, pour some olive oil and when smoking, pan-fry the split prawns for 1 minute. Add some butter and gently shake the pan so the butter coats the prawns.

Pour the prawn jus into the pan and serve in the pan at the table.

GRATED CARROTS WITH ORANGE & GINGER

Difficulty level: easy
Calories: 65
Preparation time: 15 minutes

Serves 4

200g carrots

4 tablespoons olive oil

10g freshly grated ginger

1 teaspoon brown sugar

1 orange (zest & juice)

½ lime (juice)

1 teaspoon sweet soy sauce

Salt & pepper

½ bunch coriander (chopped)

Wash, peel and grate the carrots.

In a bowl, whisk together the olive oil, ginger, sugar, orange, lime, sweet soy sauce and add salt and pepper.

In a soup plate, put some grated carrots and toss with the dressing. Sprinkle over some chopped coriander and serve.

CARROT

BIG CARROT AU JUS COOKED IN FIG LEAVES

Serves 4

Difficulty level: mediumx
Calories: 140
Preparation time: 30 minutes

50ml olive oil

8 large carrots (washed, not peeled)

Salt

500ml chicken jus

8 fig leaves

4 fresh figs (sliced)

Preheat the oven to 170°C.

In a pan, heat the olive oil until it gets really hot. Add the carrots and sauté them while making sure not to give them any colouration. We are just trying to fix their original bright colour here. Add a pinch of salt, chicken stock and cover.

After 7 minutes, remove the lid. The liquid will have almost disappeared and the carrots should be cooked. Remove the pan and let them cool down.

Meanwhile, in a greased cooking tray, line the fig leaves with the sliced fresh figs. Put a carrot on each leaf and wrap them up.

Cook in the oven for 5 minutes. The fig leaves will have turned crispy and the fresh figs will have softened over the carrots. Open up the wrapped leaves on a plate and serve.

BIG CARROT AU JUS COOKED IN FISH SKIN

Serves 4

Difficulty level: hard
Calories: 185
Preparation time: 45 minutes

50ml olive oil

8 large carrots (washed, not peeled)

Salt

500ml fish jus

8 sea bass / sea bream skins (ask your fishmonger, they are usually free)

20g butter

Follow the first part of the previous recipe but use fish jus instead of chicken jus.

After 7 minutes, remove the lid. The liquid should have almost disappeared and the carrots should be cooked. Remove the carrots from the pan and let them cool down on a dish. Lay the fish skins on a clean surface. Sprinkle some salt on them and place a carrot in the middle of each skin. Roll each carrot neatly in the fish skin.

Heat some olive oil in a large non-stick pan. When the oil looks as if it may start smoking, add the carrots rolled in fish skin. Put on low heat and slowly roll the carrots in the pan. When the fish skins start turning a little crisp, add the butter and let it turn brown. Delicately stir, making sure to coat each carrot in brown butter and serve when they all look brown and shiny.

CARROT & HONEY TART

Difficulty level: medium
Calories: 380 (for 2 helpings)
Preparation time: 6 hours

Serves 4

Tart base

250g flour

5g table salt

10g caster sugar

180g unsalted butter (cut into big squares at room temperature, softened)

1 egg

1 tablespoon water

Carrot filling

6 large carrots (peeled & cut into ½cm angled slices)

4 tablespoons good-quality liquid honey

4 eggs

40g caster sugar

2 tablespoons rum

Pinch salt

60g fresh ricotta cheese

1 teaspoon ground cumin

400ml semi-skimmed milk

200ml Activia yogurt

Making the tart base

In a bowl, mix the flour, salt, sugar and the butter by hand until you get a crumbly texture. Break in the egg and add the spoon of water. Continue working the mix until it comes together as a fragile dough.

Remove the dough from the bowl and continue working it in your hands on a floured and clean surface. Do not overwork the dough as it is always better when it is a little crumbly rather than dense and elastic.

Cover the dough with clingfilm and keep it in the fridge for at least 4 hours before using it.

Making the carrot filling

Preheat the oven to 170°C.

In a large pot, boil the carrots for 4 minutes and refresh them quickly in cold water so they retain their bright orange colour.

In a sauté pan, slowly heat up the honey and add the carrots. Stir, making sure to coat all the carrots with honey. Let the honeyed carrots cool down.

In a bowl, break the eggs, and add the sugar and the rum. Whisk them together with a pinch of salt. When the mix develops a white creamy texture, add the ricotta and the cumin. Continue whisking. Add the milk and carefully add the carrots.

With a rolling pin, flatten the dough and press it over a buttered tart mould. Fill the tart with the carrot mix and cook in the oven for 25 minutes.

Serve the tart warm with a little sour Activia yogurt.

CAULIFLOWER GRATIN

Beef jus

Difficulty level: easy
Calories: 218
Preparation time: 45 minutes

Cauliflower is a weird vegetable: it has a difficult look. I have never heard anyone looking at a cauliflower and saying: 'Oh, my God! I really need to have this now!' Children detest it and adults are rarely keen other than when they want to diversify their vegetable intake. It has an ugly shape, bad smell and it's uninspiring. It is the symbol of people refusing to eat vegetables. When I think about it, I only think about the cauliflower gratin my mother used to make. She always used condensed milk and it was the creamiest gratin I ever tasted. It was also the lightest.

Serves 4

- 2 cauliflower heads
- Salt & pepper
- 20g butter
- 20g flour
- 300ml milk
- 100ml unsweetened condensed milk
- 40g grated Cheddar
- 2 egg yolks
- Pinch mustard powder
- 20g grated Parmesan
- Pinch grated nutmeg
- Remains of roast beef jus / 100ml beef jus

Also, she used to cover the gratin with the remaining jus of a roast and that was just the most perfect thing that could happen to a tender cauliflower.

Buying the perfect cauliflower is pretty easy: its base must be very green and the flowers have to be spotless and very white.

Wash the cauliflower, making sure to have grated away any black spots.

Cut it up and cook in salted boiling water. It usually takes 4 minutes for cauliflower to be firm yet not fully cooked.

Remove the florets from the water and cool them under running water.

Heat a saucepan and melt the butter, then add the flour and let the mixture start to thicken. Add the milk and condensed milk (both cold). Cook for 3 minutes while constantly stirring and making sure that it is always gently boiling.

Remove the pan and wait until it cools down for 5 minutes.

Then add the egg yolks, mustard powder, grated parmesan, grated Cheddar and nutmeg. Add salt and pepper to taste.

Line a gratin dish with the cauliflower and cover it with the mix.

Cook in a 180°C oven for 7 minutes and add the beef jus just before serving.

CELERIAC PURÉE

Bonito flakes & lamb jus

Difficulty level: easy
Calories: 275
Preparation time: 35 minutes

I get really excited during autumn when the celeriac is at its peak. From September to December, it is a wonderful root to work with. It has deep flavour and is very versatile in terms of texture and cooking method. It can be puréed, grilled, roasted and even served raw as a slaw. It is important to be very careful when you choose celeriac. It is very often the case that a good looking celeriac may actually be empty inside. To avoid this, I usually purchase smaller celeriac and try to get them with some leaves still attached.

Serves 4

1 celeriac ball (600g)

2 small jacket potatoes (100g each)

50ml olive oil

Salt & pepper

500ml chicken broth

40g lightly salted butter

150ml lamb jus

40g breadcrumbs

4 teaspoons bonito flakes (see page 94)

The greener the leaves, the younger they are, and it is more likely that the celeriac will be full. And what makes this root even more exciting is the fact that it is very rich in vitamins A and C, minerals and is very low in calories.

Preheat the grill to 220°C.

Carefully peel the celeriac and cut it into small 2cm x 2cm cubes. Peel the potatoes and cut them the same size as the celeriac.

Heat the olive oil at low heat in a large thick-bottomed pan. Put the vegetables in and stir vigorously, making sure that the celeriac and potatoes aren't getting any colour. Add a pinch of salt and the chicken broth. Cover and cook at a slow simmer for 8 minutes.

By then, the vegetables are cooked and there should be almost no liquid left in the pan. If this is not the case, let the liquid evaporate. Remove the pan from the heat and add the butter.

Take a potato masher and mash going up and down. Do not stir or mash sideways as it may give an elastic consistency to the purée. Also do not over-mash as it is quite nice when the mash is still a little lumpy. It tends to give a bit of substance to it.

Divide the celeriac mash into four soup plates. Meanwhile, reheat the lamb jus and pour some on top of each plate. Sprinkle on the breadcrumbs and put on the highest tray of the oven (grill position) for 3 minutes, so the breadcrumbs get a nice golden-brown colour.

Remove from the oven and sprinkle some bonito flakes to accentuate the umami flavour of the dish.

Serve immediately.

PIGGY CELERIAC

Difficulty level: hard
Calories: 280
Preparation time: 1 hour 30 minutes

Serves 4

- 2 small celeriac
- 18 slices maple-glazed bacon (or pancetta, or smoked streaky bacon)
- 50ml olive oil
- 1 onion (peeled & diced)
- 1 shallot (peeled & diced)
- 1 very pale celery stalk (washed & diced)
- 100ml red wine
- 200ml chicken broth
- 20g butter
- 180g girolles (washed, grated & pre-sautéed to remove excess water)

Peel and wash the celeriac, making sure that you keep them whole. Boil in salted water for 15 minutes. Do make sure that the celeriac are cooked but retain a little tenderness. Refresh and dry them out.

Take two slices of bacon and cut them into small strips. With a small knife, insert the slices inside the celeriac. Be careful not to break the celeriac, and try to go as deep as possible.

Wrap the celeriac in the remaining slices of bacon. You can tie them up with string to make sure that the bacon will stick to the celeriac during the remaining cooking process.

Preheat the oven to 170°C.

In a small sauté pan, heat some olive oil and add the diced onion, shallots and celery.

Stir and add the red wine. Let the red wine evaporate for 1 minute, then place both celeriac on top of the garnish. Add the chicken broth. Remove the pan from the stove and put in the oven for 40 minutes.

Turn the celeriac every 10 minutes, so the cooking is even.

Just before taking the celeriac out of the oven, heat some butter in a sauté pan. When the butter turns brown, add the girolles and quickly pan-fry them for less than a minute. Add salt and pepper, and add them to the celeriac dish.

Serve the dish and carve the celeriac at the table.

Chicory can be white or red. The white is usually more bitter than the red. I like doing a cure of chicory at the beginning of each year. I eat it raw before every meal. On top of making me chew like crazy, it also makes me visit the loo more often than usual.

I clean the inside of my body for a good start to the year.

Chicory connoisseurs are usually tempted by the ones from the end of the season when the yellow chicory turns green and slightly curly. It is the perfect bitter vegetable.

CHICORY

GRILLED CHICORY

Consommé of peppered leaves & sautéed chanterelles

Difficulty level: medium
Calories: 110
Preparation time: 1 hour

Serves 4

2 red chicory

2 white chicory

50ml olive oil

40g butter

½ leek (finely chopped)

80g clean chanterelles

Salt

500ml water

½ bunch sorrel

½ bunch flat-leaf parsley (chopped)

Black pepper

Start by choosing the hardest chicory you can find, then slice them lengthways and remove the tough part near the top of the slice. Dip them in olive oil and quickly grill them until they become almost black and slightly soft. Some of the leaves will turn crispy.

Into a large heated pan, add the butter. When it turns brown, throw in the leeks and mushrooms and stir vigorously. Add a pinch of salt. When the mushrooms start releasing their moisture, pour over the water and bring to the boil.

Prepare the sorrel by removing the leaves from the stem. Wash them and add the leaves to the chanterelle water. Cook for 1 minute at a slow simmer.

Serve this dish by putting the slices of chicory in the middle of the plate, scatter the flat-leaf parsley around, grind some pepper and pour the stock together with the mushrooms over it.

CHICORY

BRAISED CHESTNUTS & WHITE CHICORY

Difficulty level: medium
Calories: 170
Preparation time: 1 hour

Serves 4

- 6 white chicory
- 80g butter
- 150g vacuum-packed chestnuts
- Salt
- 100ml olive oil
- 200ml chicken jus
- Pepper

Wash the chicory and dry them with a kitchen cloth. Cut the chicory into thick slices and keep them on a plate covered with clingfilm (so they don't turn black). Heat some butter in a large pot and add the chestnuts when it turns brown. Stir and add salt. When the chestnuts are slightly caramelised, put the slices of chicory on top, making sure that none touch the bottom of the pan. Add a bit of water and salt. Cover and cook slowly for 15 minutes. Check often whether the amount of water is sufficient to create steam for the chicory to cook. Remove the slices of chicory when they are cooked and put them in a gratin dish. Place the chestnuts on top (they should be smashed by then) and add the olive oil, the chicken jus and some black pepper. Serve hot.

WHITE CHICORY SALAD WITH BLUE CHEESE, BACON, GRANNY SMITH & TOASTED ALMOND *(Pictured overleaf)*

Difficulty level: easy
Calories: 235
Preparation time: 30 minutes

Serves 4

- 1 egg yolk
- 1 tablespoon Dijon mustard
- 100ml grapeseed oil
- 2 tablespoons red wine vinegar
- 1 lemon (zest & juice)
- Salt & pepper
- 2 boiled eggs (peeled)
- 4 white chicory
- 4 slices smoked streaky bacon
- 40g flaked almonds
- 2 Granny Smith apples (cored & thinly sliced)
- 100g blue cheese (crumbled into small pieces)
- 50ml olive oil

Start by making the dressing. Whisk an egg yolk with the mustard and emulsify it by slowly adding the grapeseed oil. Add the red wine vinegar, lemon juice, salt and pepper. Taste and add the boiled eggs. Mash them up with a fork so they give a real consistency to the dressing. Reserve for later use.

Detach the chicory leaves from the bases and wash them thoroughly under very cold water. Dry them carefully with a clean cloth. Then cut them in two lengthways.

Put a non-stick pan on high heat and pan-fry the slices of bacon for 2 minutes on each side. Add the flaked almonds and sauté them with the bacon for 30 seconds. Remove from the pan. Toss the chicory in a bowl with the dressing.

Divide the chicory between 4 large plates and add the bacon, almonds, grated lemon zest, slices of apple and crumbled blue cheese. Add a drizzle of olive oil and serve.

COURGETTE

The courgette is very easy to digest and contains only 17 calories for every 100g eaten. It is super-rich in water and potassium and very low in sodium. I have heard people say that it is a very calming vegetable and it is sometimes administered as a cure for hyper-active kids!

When I was working in California as a private chef, I was able to pick some vegetables from the garden behind the house. My favourite ingredient was the courgette flower.

Catherina, the garden boss, couldn't understand why I was removing the flowers of her courgettes. What was the point? she always asked me.

I just wanted to stuff them or to mix them in a salad.

We were in the early 1990s and this was a sort of nouvelle cuisine that she couldn't understand. The courgette flower is now very expensive, and quite popular. If you feel like having some, I would recommend eating them raw in salad, because stuffing the courgette flower is probably the single item that represents for me what nouvelle cuisine was all about.

Times are changing and the courgette is now eaten early in its season as a vegetable rather than as a flower. So that is good.

In order to recognise a good courgette you need to make sure that it is heavy and the skin has to be thin, shiny and spotless. It can be small, long, round, short or even twisted. A good courgette, just like a tomato, should feel heavy in hand to taste good.

MARINATED COURGETTES & LIME
Scottish scallops and jalapeño pepper

Difficulty level: medium
Calories: 85
Preparation time: 2 hours 30 minutes

Courgettes are just like your most boring friend. An absolute bore when on their own! But as soon as you add a combination of texture, flavour and presentation, they suddenly turn into the perfect partner. They are not going to change your life, but they will definitely become part of it. This dish is the perfect example.

Serves 4

- 2 large courgettes
- 2 limes
- Salt & pepper
- 10 tablespoons olive oil
- ½ shallot
- ½ garlic clove
- ¼ red pepper
- ¼ tiny jalapeño pepper
- ½ lemon
- 2 tablespoons white wine vinegar
- 1 tablespoon soy sauce
- 4 scallops

For the courgettes

Wash the courgettes and slice them as thinly as you can (about 3mm thick) with a very sharp, long knife (so the courgette won't crack or break).

Put them in a bowl with the juice of one lime, salt, pepper and 4 spoons of olive oil.

Cover the bowl with clingfilm and refrigerate for at least 2 hours.

Making the marinade

Chop the shallot, garlic clove, red pepper and jalapeño pepper into tiny little cubes and put them in a vegetable bowl.

Add the juice of the other lime and half a lemon. Add the white wine vinegar, soy sauce, the remaining olive oil, salt and black pepper and stir.

Slice the scallops flat, the same thickness as the courgettes.

On a large round plate, make a courgette rosette, alternating with smaller rosettes of thinly sliced scallops.

Pour the marinade over and serve.

COURGETTE & MINT GRANITÉ

Difficulty level: medium
Calories: 80 calories
Preparation time: 3 hours

My kids categorically refused to be fed courgette. Nothing I could do. I tried to hide it everywhere: in purée under a steak, mixed in soup with mint, mixed with rice . . . I even attempted the unforgivable: a courgette pizza! Nothing ever worked until I decided to try it with sweet things. Suddenly I realised that courgette could give some sort of body to a simple granité or sorbet. I tried and it worked. So now when I am asked if my kids eat everything, I proudly say YES! Even courgettes!

Serves 4

750g courgettes

1 bunch Corsican mint (or common mint if you can't get Corsican)

80g sugar

500ml water

1 lime (juice)

Wash the courgettes and remove both ends. Grate the courgette skins against a cheese grater. Keep the grated skins in a bowl (I know it will look really mashed!) and chop the rest of the courgette in a food processor with the mint leaves. This will turn into a bright-green lumpy juice.

Put the juice in a saucepan and add the sugar and the water. Bring it to the boil and let it cool. When the mixture is almost cold, add the mashed green skin and put in the freezer.

Scratch the top of the ice with a fork every 2 hours in order to get a perfect granité texture.

You can serve it as a starter or a pudding with a splash of lime juice.

OVEN-BAKED COURGETTES

Confit tomatoes

Difficulty level: easy
Calories: 90
Preparation time: 90 minutes

After many years of eating and cooking watery vegetables, I can happily say that when they are simply cooked with olive oil in a pot they are absolutely wonderful. But the moment they are finished with a bit of thyme and Parmesan they take on another dimension. Their original flavour is suddenly enhanced. It is like watching a film in 2D and suddenly seeing it in 3D. Sense-popping!

Serves 4

- 800g ripe plum tomatoes
- 3 tablespoons olive oil
- 1 garlic clove
- Salt
- Black pepper
- 1 tablespoon sugar
- 4 sprigs fresh thyme (lemon thyme can also be used)
- 600g courgettes (fattest you can find)
- 2 tablespoons grated Parmesan

Preheat the oven to 120°C.

Remove the peduncle of each tomato and wash them under very cold water for 20 seconds. Drain and dry. Cut them in ½cm-thick slices.

Put some olive oil in a large roasting tray and rub the garlic clove over it.

Line slices of tomato in the dish and add salt, pepper, sugar and a little fresh thyme.

Sprinkle on a bit of olive oil and put in the oven for 10 minutes.

After 10 minutes, open the oven door slightly – you can use a wooden spoon to prevent the door from closing fully. Let the tomatoes dehydrate and concentrate their taste for a further 30 minutes.

Meanwhile wash the courgettes and cut them into ½cm-thick slices.

Put them in a vegetable bowl and toss in olive oil with salt and pepper.

When the tomatoes are ready, alternate them with the courgettes in a pot. Sprinkle over the Parmesan and the remaining thyme.

Put the oven to grill position and finish with a little grilling of the Parmesan and thyme tops.

Serve very hot. You will be amazed by the smell of thyme, Parmesan and tomato gratin. So memorable!

COURGETTE, AUBERGINE & SAFFRON CREAM

Difficulty level: medium
Calories: 150
Preparation time: 30 minutes

Some ingredients just seem to always work when they are paired together. They usually complement each other because of the contrast they apply to each other: tomato and onion, artichoke and truffle, basil and garlic, brown butter and lemon . . . One of the weirdest perfect combinations is the one between courgette and aubergine. Bluntly speaking, they are two weak vegetables. A bit too watery to balance each other, you would think. It just goes to show that vegetables are unpredictable and we should never assume anything.

Serves 4

500g courgettes

500g aubergines

1 red pepper

Olive oil

Salt & pepper

1 tablespoon caster sugar

500ml whipping cream

1g saffron

1 glass water

Wash and cut the courgettes, aubergines and red pepper into small cubes.

Pour some olive oil into a large flat pan and fry the cubes, making sure to stir vigorously so it doesn't burn at the base of the pan. Add salt, pepper and a tablespoon of sugar.

Continue stirring until the cubes start caramelising. Add the cream and saffron. Stir and add the glass of water.

Cover and cook at a slow simmer for 10 minutes.

Do not drain. Liquidise the soup so it turns creamy.

Correct the seasoning if needed and serve very hot with a dollop of cream and a few saffron strands.

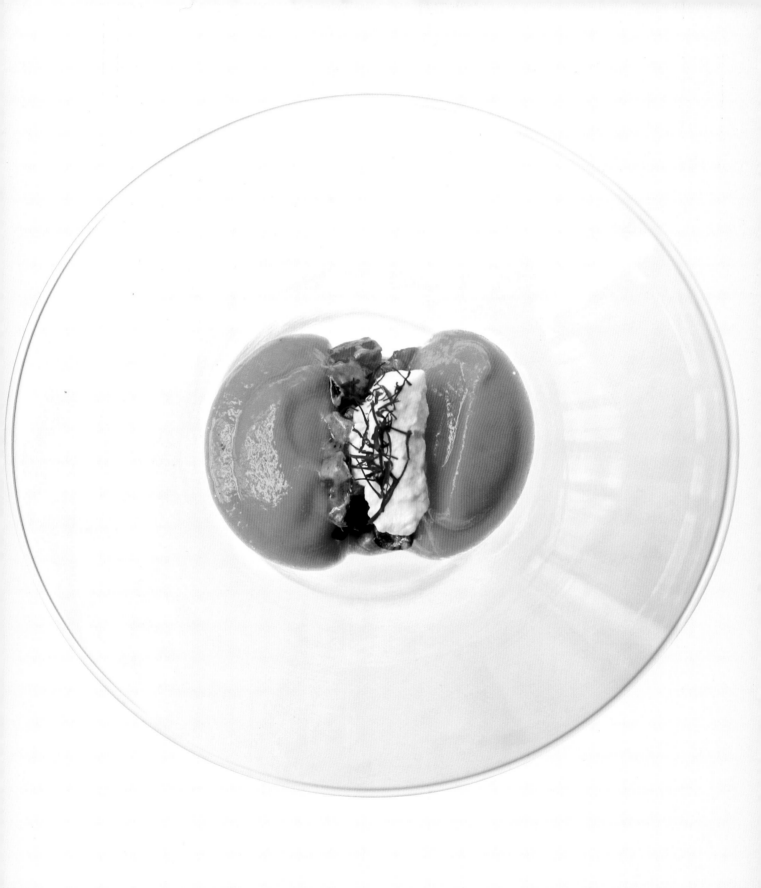

CUCUMBER, GINGER & TARRAGON

Difficulty level: easy
Calories: 172
Preparation time: 30 minutes

Cucumber is famous for being the worst vegetable to digest and on top of that it is one of the most tasteless. It is also the only vegetable my chefs can't stop playing with every time I get some delivered. Boys will always be boys! Personally, I love its shape, its very particular flavour and its texture. I also like the fact that cucumber is rich in water and that it's very good if you are, like me, constantly trying to lose some extra kilos. I use cucumber both cooked and raw and use it mostly in the summer.

Serves 6

- 2 tablespoons sesame oil
- Salt & pepper
- 2 garlic cloves (minced)
- 1 tablespoon caster sugar
- 2 tablespoons tarragon / red wine vinegar
- 2 large cucumbers (peeled & cut into 5cm-long strips)
- 60g fresh ginger (peeled & minced)
- ½ bunch tarragon (roughly chopped)
- ½ tablespoon white sesame seeds
- ½ tablespoon black sesame seeds

When dressed with vinegar and sugar, cucumber shines by the power it has to combine two very strong flavours.

When it is served with a chilled and refreshing summer crustacean broth, cucumber tempers the power of prawns, plus it also brings a vegetable aspect to the dish.

Into a large pot, pour the sesame oil, a pinch of salt, garlic, pepper, sugar and a bit of tarragon vinegar. Then add the cucumber and bring to the boil. Remove immediately from the heat.

When the cucumbers are cold, transfer them to a bowl and cover with the fresh ginger. Toss until they are well coated, then add the fresh tarragon.

Sprinkle on some sesame seeds.

If used to accompany an aperitif, I usually plant a small wooden stick in each cucumber baton to facilitate the serving. Serve very cold.

CUCUMBER, ROCKET, MINT & CHILLED PRAWN BROTH

Difficulty level: hard
Calories: 160
Preparation time: 30 minutes

Serves 4

60g black radishes

2 large cucumbers

16 small pre-cooked prawns

½ bunch fresh mint

50ml olive oil

Salt & pepper

100g rocket leaves

1 litre prawn broth (chilled)

100ml whipping cream (whisked until almost firm & kept in the fridge until serving)

Peel the black radishes and cut crossways to get some very small and thin slices. Keep the slices in cold water in the fridge until serving.

Peel the cucumber neatly, making sure that the entire skin has been perfectly removed.

With a small, sharp knife, cut some small pieces of cucumber, ½cm thick. Keep them in very cold water until serving.

Peel the pre-cooked prawns and put them in a large bowl. Chop some mint leaves and toss in with the prawns and the olive oil, salt and pepper. Then add the wild rocket leaves and toss again, making sure that the leaves are well coated with oil.

Into 4 soup plates, divide the cucumber pieces and top them with the slices of black radish and wild rocket leaves. Arrange the prawns and place the remaining mint leaves over each plate.

Pour the broth on top and add a small dollop of whipped cream.

SOFT FENNEL SALAD

Lemon, parsley & yogurt sorbet

Difficulty level: medium
Calories: 150
Preparation time: 2 hours

Serves 6

Fennel

4 fennel bulbs

Sorbet

600ml water

400g sugar

2 lemons (zest)

½ bunch parsley

600ml lemon juice

300ml yogurt

Dressing

2 tablespoons mirin

2 tablespoons caster sugar

2 tablespoons soy sauce

1 tablespoon balsamic vinegar

8 tablespoons olive oil

Preparing the fennel

Wash the fennel and cut away any black stains from the skins. Cut them in 2 and thinly slice them with a mandolin. Put them in icy cold water for 10 minutes until they become crunchy. Dry them with a cloth.

Making the sorbet

Prepare the sorbet by bringing the water, sugar and lemon zest to the boil.

Liquidise the parsley and add it to the lemon syrup and yogurt. Turn in an ice cream machine.

Making the dressing

In a bowl mix the mirin, caster sugar, soy sauce, balsamic vinegar and olive oil.

Serving the dish

Gently add the fennel slices to the dressing.

Divide between 4 plates and add some spoons of the sorbet.

FENNEL & EGG GRATIN

Lamb jus & thyme

Difficulty level: medium
Calories: 380
Preparation time: 1 hour

Serves 4

- 8 fennel bulbs (outer dark leaves removed & washed)
- 100ml olive oil
- Salt & pepper
- 500ml chicken stock
- 2 egg yolks
- 200ml double cream
- 40g grated Cheddar
- 12 eggs (boiled for 10 minutes, peeled & sliced with an egg slicer)
- 200ml lamb jus
- 3 sprigs thyme

Preheat the grill to 190°C.

Cut the fennel lengthways in 2, then slice across about 1cm thick.

In a large sauté pan, heat the olive oil until very hot. Add the slices of fennel, salt and turn them around while giving them a little colouration. Add the chicken stock and cover. Cook for 6 minutes at high heat. Check if the fennel is cooked by inserting a knife into the bright white part of it. If there is no resistance, it means that the fennel is properly cooked.

Remove the fennel from the cooking pan. Transfer the cooking liquid into a bowl and add the egg yolks, cream and grated Cheddar. Taste and add salt and pepper if needed.

Line a buttered roasting dish with the slices of fennel. Cover with slices of boiled egg. Add the fennel juice mixed with the egg yolk and cheese. Pour the lamb jus over the dish and sprinkle with thyme.

Cook under the grill for 4 to 5 minutes, until the dish looks golden-brown.

Remove from the oven and serve immediately.

GARLIC

Garlic is one of the most ancient condiments we can find. It was used in China for its magical virtues. In Egypt, garlic was given to pyramid builders to prevent them from disease and to provide them with extra strength. Good for the builders but bad for the Pharaohs, who banned garlic from their court because of its smell.

In Paris, people used to eat garlic on toast with butter because they thought that it was good for them. They didn't mind that garlic is hard to digest and not exactly great for social occasions because of your breath after eating it.

Garlic can be eaten raw or cooked. It can be cooked as a vegetable but is known primarily as a flavouring.

I was brought up in a garlic world. Garlic was everywhere around me. Meat cooked with garlic stuffed in every hole, fish wrapped in garlic leaves, garlic and bread soup during winter, garlic and milk when I was sick, and my mother's kisses before going to bed which always smelled of a combination of garlic and blue Gauloise cigarettes.

CHILLED BROAD BEAN & GARLIC SOUP *Ricotta cheese*

Difficulty level: medium
Calories: 230
Preparation time: 30 minutes Resting: 4 hours

It is common knowledge in the South of France that you recognise good garlic and how wonderful it tastes when you burp it. A garlic tsunami submerging your entire nose and tastebuds is something you would look for. This recipe should not be served before important business meetings or romantic gatherings, but for garlic lovers this is heaven.

Serves 4

- 2kg fresh broad beans
- 2 garlic heads
- Olive oil
- Salt & pepper
- 3 litres water
- 100ml single cream
- 80g fresh ricotta cheese

Divide the volume of broad beans in 2.

With the first kilo:

Chop 1kg of broad beans (in their pods) to 1cm thick. Wash under running water for 5 minutes to make sure that all possible dirt is removed.

Peel the garlic heads (retaining a couple of garlic cloves for presentation) and smash the cloves flat on a board with your hand. Pour some olive oil into a pan. When the oil is hot, add the garlic, making sure that it isn't coloured.

Add the chopped broad beans and stir vigorously. Make sure not to give any colouration (by doing so you will intensify the bright green colour of the soup). When the broad beans are very shiny, add some salt, water and single cream. Cover with a lid and cook for 12 minutes.

Blitz in a mixer for 10 minutes and pass through a large-holed sieve. The soup should have a creamy texture. If it is too thick, add a bit of single cream mixed with salted water. Keep in the fridge for at least 4 hours before serving.

With the second kilo:

First, peel some garlic cloves, slice them and slowly deep-fry them in oil so they become slightly crunchy and a little bitter. Double peel the broad beans, making sure to remove every layer of skin. Once this is done, put them into a bowl and season with salt, pepper and olive oil.

Place the broad beans at the bottom of the soup plate and add a spoonful of fresh ricotta cheese in each plate. Season the ricotta with some salt, black pepper and olive oil. Sprinkle the fried slices of garlic onto the dish.

Pour the very cold soup around and serve.

BAMBOO STEAMED COD

Wrapped in garlic leaves, golden croûtons & Cos lettuce

Difficulty level: hard
Calories: 265
Preparation time: 45 minutes

Wild garlic picking is like truffle hunting. When you know where to find it, you never share it with anybody. I know half a dozen very special woods by the sea where I can pick some delicious garlic leaves during its season. The Isle of Wight, for example, has some immense undiscovered fields of garlic leaves that appear from late February and disappear by the end of March. You have to look hard to find the perfect spot, but once found, it is like discovering a pot of gold. Little things like that make one feel so important sometimes.

Serves 4

400g fresh cod fillet

Salt & pepper

20 garlic leaves

2 slices white bread

10g butter

2 Cos lettuce

1 garlic clove

1 tablespoon aged balsamic vinegar

4 tablespoons olive oil

You will need a Chinese-style bamboo steamer for this recipe.

Cut the fillet of cod into 4 slices.

Season each piece with a little salt and black pepper.

Wrap in 4 garlic leaves and place inside a closed Chinese bamboo steamer.

Cut the slices of white bread into small cubes and pan-fry in butter.

Cut at the base of the lettuce to release the leaves, and wash under running water.

Chop the garlic clove very thinly and combine with the balsamic vinegar, 3 spoonfuls of olive oil and salt and pepper. Taste and correct if needed.

In a sauté pan, boil 2cm deep of water with 4 garlic leaves. Place the bamboo steamer in the pan and steam the fish for 5 minutes.

Meanwhile, toss the Cos lettuce in the dressing and add the fried croûtons.

Place lettuce and croûtons in the middle of each serving plate and top with a wrapped fish.

Serve immediately.

GARLIC

AIGO BOULIDO

Difficulty level: medium
Calories: 160
Preparation time: 45 minutes

Serves 4

- 4 garlic heads (1 head per person)
- 2 litres water
- 4 sage leaves
- 1 bay leaf
- 1 tablespoon sea salt
- Olive oil
- Black pepper
- 4 slices of Pain de Campagne (preferably a little old)
- ½ bunch flat-leaf parsley (roughly chopped)

This translates as boiled garlic from Provençe.

Peel the garlic and remove the gems within the clove. Cook them in 2 litres of water with the sage, bay leaf and salt until the garlic is soft (around 15 minutes).

Then remove the garlic from the stock and mash it in a bowl with a fork. Add a little olive oil so it gets the consistency of a paste. Add a pinch of salt and some black pepper.

Let the stock reduce for an extra 15 minutes. Pass it through a sieve and season to taste.

Cut the bread into 4cm x 4cm squares and add a spoon of olive oil on each piece of bread. Toast the bread in a toaster or under the grill.

Top the bread with the garlic paste and plae each piece in a soup bowl. Add some roughly chopped flat-leaf parsley, black pepper and pour the garlic broth over.

Eat when very hot with a large splash of olive oil.

GARLIC JAM

Difficulty level: easy
Calories: 50
Preparation time: 1 hour

Serves 4

- 30g garlic cloves (peeled)
- 200ml condensed milk
- 10g sugar
- Salt & pepper

Remove the gems in the garlic cloves and put the cloves in a pot filled with the condensed milk, sugar, salt and pepper. Cook slowly until you get a thick paste.

Put this paste in the fridge and serve it on toasted bread as an appetiser (or for breakfast).

GARLIC PESTO DIP

Difficulty level: easy
Calories: 210
Preparation time: 30 minutes

There are two things you must accept the day you decide to start being taken seriously as a cook (home or restaurant). The first one is that your nails will never look the same as before (never trust a chef with clean nails. He surely hasn't cooked for years). The second is that your hands will always smell of garlic. It is one of those smells that you can never really get rid of. When mixed with human skin, it penetrates and lingers even after days of intense washing.

Serves 4

150g wild garlic leaves

1 garlic head

½ bunch flat-leaf parsley

45g toasted cashew nuts

30g finely grated Parmesan

1 small red chilli

125ml olive oil

Salt & pepper

1 tablespoon white wine vinegar

Bunch small carrots (peeled)

Place the garlic leaves, peeled garlic, flat-leaf parsley leaves, cashew nuts and Parmesan in a mortar and pound until well combined.

Finely seed and chop the red chilli and add to the mixture.

Gradually add the oil in a thin and steady stream.

You need to make sure that it turns into a thick paste. Taste and add salt, pepper and the white wine vinegar.

Transfer to an airtight container and pour over a little extra oil to cover the pesto surface.

Serve the pesto with some little raw vegetable sticks such as carrot, celery, white chard or crunchy lettuce leaves.

LEEK

Winter or spring, the leek is one of the most important vegetables we can find in a kitchen. It is a basic ingredient in many preparations: stock, juice, soup and much more.

It is also one of the oldest vegetables. The Egyptians loved it so much that they considered it a flower and used to give it as a present to good soldiers. In the Roman Empire, the leek was reputed to clear your voicebox. Nero used to eat a lot before his long and famous speeches. The Romans introduced the leek to Great Britain and then the leek became the emblem of Wales.

We know that the leek is very rich in potassium, vitamins K and A, and is an excellent diuretic. In my kitchen the leek is almost everywhere, especially in winter when it becomes hard to find a bit of green in vegetables. What gives me the most pleasure is to make it shine on its own. Leek doesn't need much help from any other ingredient or even any dressing.

The complexity of its texture makes it most interesting to work with. The leek is a complicated vegetable with thin layers of juicy tenderness in a shade of green. Steamed, boiled, pan-fried or even deep-fried are just a few ways you can get the best of this kitchen pearl.

If this isn't enough to convince you that leek is far superior as an ingredient to fillet of beef, for example, you should remember that it is the perfect tool if you need to lose weight. Stuff yourself with leeks every day for a long period and you will see how your body changes.

My grandmother made it an annual ritual to feed herself solely with leeks for the first months of each year. She would then lose the extra kilos. She would serve them warm in a not-too-sweet and sour dressing.

This is most definitely the easiest way to fall in love with leeks.

SOFT LEEK

Yogurt vinaigrette, boiled egg, capers & anchovies

Difficulty level: medium
Calories: 90
Preparation time: 15 minutes

In this dish it is not the leek that brings its light and fresh fibrous texture for the anchovy to shine. It is completely the opposite. The whole dish is built around the soft texture of the leek and the other ingredients are mainly to make the leek look and taste even better without compromising its own specific refinement. Take a mouthful of all the ingredients and you'll see how they all play around the leek.

Serves 4

4 large leeks

100ml olive oil

Salt

4 eggs

1 tablespoon Dijon mustard

1 tablespoon red wine vinegar

Pepper

1 small tub Activia yogurt

12 small anchovy fillets

30g capers

Remove the darkest green part of the leek. If you buy your leeks from a supermarket, it may already be removed. Cut the leeks in half, lengthways and wash them. Do not be afraid to open them up in order to wash everywhere.

As with most green vegetables, you will be cooking the leeks by heating a bit of olive oil in a pan. When the oil is smoking, put the leeks in and shake the pan without flaming it until you have stabilised their chlorophyll without colouration. Add salt, water and cover. Check often.

When the leeks are tender, remove the lid and let the juices evaporate. Then remove them and place in a large dish with the rest of the olive oil.

Cook the eggs in boiling water for 8 minutes. Peel them under running water (to make it easier).

Into a large bowl, put the mustard, vinegar, salt and pepper and start whisking while pouring in the yogurt. Taste constantly until you think that the balance of acidity to sweetness is perfect for your taste.

Place the leeks face up on each plate. Add the anchovy fillets and sprinkle over some capers.

Mash the boiled eggs while still warm. Then pour the vinaigrette over the leeks and top with the boiled eggs.

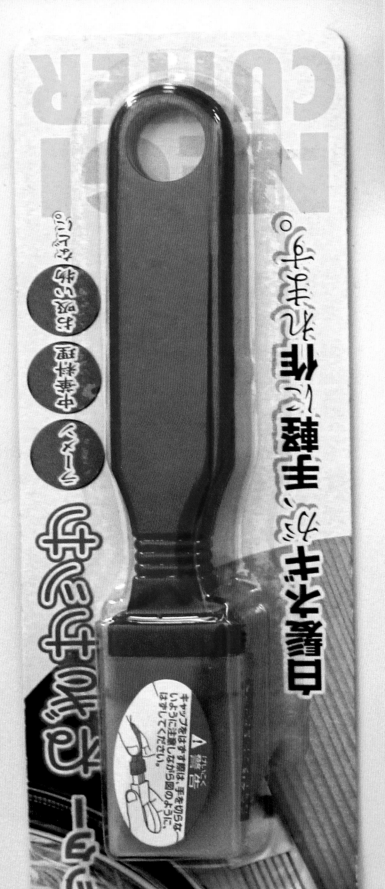

STAINLESS STEEL

GRA

お手頃!!
コンパクト

ステ

薬味お

ちょっとおろした
い時にお手頃サイ
ズ。わさび、にん
にく、しょうが等
少量おろせます。

STAINLESS STEEL
JAPAN

LEEK

GREEN LEEK JAM

Difficulty level: easy
Calories: 105
Preparation time: 45 minutes

Serves 4

200g leeks

40g butter

1 lime (chopped)

Indonesian pepper

2 tablespoons sugar

150ml water

Wash and dry the leeks (especially the green ends).

In a large saucepan, heat the butter. When it turns brown, add the leeks, the lime, the Indonesian pepper and the sugar. Cover with water and slowly cook for 20 minutes.

Serve cold. It is superb with grilled fish!

LEEK, TRUFFLE & BONITO

Difficulty level: hard
Calories: 55
Preparation time: 30 minutes

Serves 4

20 small leeks

2 teaspoons Dijon mustard

2 tablespoons red wine vinegar

8 tablespoons sunflower oil

2 teaspoons black truffle oil

Salt & pepper

40g black Perigord truffle

2 teaspoons bonito flakes (see page 94)

Delicately clean the leeks by removing the dark and hard end parts. Also, remove their first skin which is usually a little sticky.

In a bowl, combine the Dijon mustard and the red wine vinegar and start whisking slowly while adding the sunflower oil. Finish by adding the truffle oil, salt and pepper.

Boil the leeks in salted water for 4 minutes. Drain and dry them as much as you can with a clean towel.

Place five leeks on each plate, add a few slices of black truffle on top and pour the vinaigrette around. The leeks should be warm to be really enjoyed.

Sprinkle a few bonito flakes as you serve to accentuate the flavour of the truffle.

FONDANT LENTILS

Black & round radishes, leaves & mustard dressing

Difficulty level: medium
Calories: 230
Preparation time: 45 minutes

The lentil is a most nutritious ingredient. It is one of my favourite vegetables. I could eat lentils every day, all year long. Lentils are a great source of minerals and are rich in calcium, potassium, zinc and folic acid. They are also perfect if you are looking to lose weight (well, as long as you only eat lentils). Lentils are considered a winter vegetable but I always argue against that point since I eat them all year round. I like them in winter as a lentil soup and in summer in a cold salad with chopped shallots and honey dressing.

Serves 4

- 100g dried green lentils
- ½ onion
- ½ leek (halved & washed)
- ½ carrot
- 1 bay leaf
- Pinch whole black pepper
- 1 tablespoon sea salt
- 1 teaspoon Dijon mustard
- 1 tablespoon red wine vinegar
- 100ml olive oil
- 1 bunch round radishes (keep the leaves)
- ½ black radish

Place the lentils in a cooking pot and fill it with water. Bring to the boil, drain and run under water until cold.

Put the lentils back in the pot and fill it with water, ½ an onion (not chopped), the leek, the carrot, bay leaf and one pinch of black pepper. Cook at a very slow simmer.

Taste every 5 to 10 minutes until the lentils are almost melting between your teeth. You will, at this moment, realise that they are very under salted. As with beans, if you salt during the cooking process, the lentils tend to break. It is just a matter of keeping the shape of the lentils intact. But on the other hand if you aren't bothered about that, then salt them as you put the garnishes on and rectify before serving.

In a bowl, whisk the Dijon mustard with the red wine vinegar and olive oil. Add some salt and pepper and taste.

On a plate, pour a few spoonfuls of cooked lentils with a bit of their cooking stock. Place the radish leaves (washed) with some thin slices of black radish over the lentils. Then top with thinly sliced round radishes and pour over the dressing.

BREADCRUMBED TOFU & LENTILS *Sweet basil & chilli dressing*

Difficulty level: medium
Calories: 210
Preparation time: 45 minutes

I had a dream. A dream of making my children salivate when they saw tofu. A dream of seeing them ask for more. More tofu, please! Their natural reaction was total revulsion. They didn't like its look, its taste and its texture even less. However, after eating this dish of breadcrumbed tofu with basil, lentils and shallots they have turned out to be completely hooked!

Serves 4

- 100g cooked lentils (as in the previous recipe)
- 1 long shallot (peeled and thinly sliced)
- 1 bunch sweet Thai basil (chopped)
- ½ small chilli (finely chopped)
- 100ml olive oil
- 2 tablespoons balsamic vinegar
- Salt & pepper
- 1 egg
- 2 tablespoons fresh milk
- 1 block firm tofu
- 50g breadcrumbs

Cold, cooked lentils are perfect for this.

Put the lentils in a large bowl with thinly sliced shallots, chopped Thai basil leaves, chilli, olive oil, balsamic vinegar, salt and pepper. Stir to get a tasty dressing mixed with the lentils.

Break an egg into a soup plate and mix in the milk. Dip the tofu in it and then transfer the tofu to another plate and cover it with breadcrumbs. In a frying pan, heat one spoonful of olive oil. When smoking, put the tofu in the pan and make sure that it cooks quickly without sticking to the bottom of the pan. After 2 minutes, remove it and put it on a cutting board. Slice it thickly and put the dressed lentils in between.

Put the tofu slices in the fridge for a couple of hours and serve cold with a large splash of olive oil on top, some more chopped basil and a few drops of balsamic vinegar.

A SLIMMING PUNISHMENT

Simple and delicious punishments for having put on so much weight. A remedy for fatness.

SLIMMING LENTIL COCKTAIL

Difficulty level: easy
Calories: 80
Preparation time: 10 minutes

Serves 1

50g cooked lentils (cold)

60ml soya milk

1 tablespoon white wine vinegar

100ml water

In the bowl of a large blender blitz all the ingredients for 3 minutes until you get a smooth consistency.

Don't expect this drink to look like your favourite triple-fat frappuccino. This is all about filling you up with lentils!

THE JUS OF A ROSEVAL

Difficulty level: easy
Calories: 150
Preparation time: 20 minutes

Serves 1

200g Roseval (red skin) potatoes

1 tablespoon honey

Peel the potatoes. Rub them against a cheese grater. Keep the juice and throw the rest away. You can add a spoonful of honey if you feel a bit disgusted by the cat's tongue feeling in your mouth.

CARROT & ALOE VERA COLON CLEANSER

Difficulty level: easy
Calories: 35
Preparation time: 10 minutes

Serves 1

1 lemon (juice)

1 large carrot (peeled & grated)

100ml pure aloe vera water

Pinch salt

You won't be on the road to rejuvenation unless you drink this delicious day-starter. No need for me to go into details of the wonderful consequence this drink will have on your digestion. The title says it all!

Warm the juice of one lemon. Add it to the bowl of a blender with the grated carrot, aloe vera water and pinch of salt.

Blitz and drink straight after. Don't leave your house for the next 20 minutes.

WILD MUS

Buying them from the market is the safest thing to do when it comes to wild mushrooms. The best thing is to actually get used to them in the market and then try to recognise them when wood walking for mushrooms.

Wild mushrooms are seasonal produce that are easy to use and to cook. They also bring a real depth of flavour to dishes. Their nuttiness and mineral flavour can be enhanced by either meat or fish jus.

They are real stars in my kitchen and are treated like royalty.

I would classify wild mushrooms in this order:

Cèp: many sorts of cèpes exist. The best ones are the brown or bronze cèpes. The 'tete-de-negre' is not bad either. They are available in late summer and autumn. They have their own section from page 200.

Chanterelle: most commonly known as 'girolle', this is my favourite wild mushroom. When cooked with brown butter it tastes divine.

Mousseron: the mousseron is in season during the months of April, May and June only. It tastes fantastic when served with white dandelion leaves. It is almost bitter. In the mouth, it becomes almost sweet, thanks to the nutty and sweet butter they are usually tossed in.

Morel: too expensive and too good, they come in spring with the asparagus and are their best partner. Morel has to be eaten alone or with green vegetables such as green peas, broad beans, asparagus, sautéed Cos lettuce or simply with a meat jus.

LIGHTLY CRUMBED MORELS

Veal jus, garlic & parsley

Difficulty level: medium
Calories: 330
Preparation time: 1 hour

This wild spring mushroom is probably the most exquisite mushroom a chef can cook with. Unlike truffles, which need to be served raw to be fully appreciated, morels need to be cooked to get the best of their texture and flavour. The grey-brown heads are conical, chambered and have small wrinkles. Because morels contain less water than other varieties of wild mushrooms, they require liquid when cooked. You can therefore easily imagine that morels are perfect when combined with chicken or veal jus.

Serves 4

60g unsalted butter

1 shallot (finely diced)

4 garlic cloves (smashed & finely chopped)

300g fresh morels (washed 3 times to make sure that no sand is left in its pores)

Salt

200ml double cream

100ml chicken jus

80g Japanese breadcrumbs (they are very light; you can also use ordinary ones)

10g clarified butter

½ bunch flat-leaf parsley (roughly chopped)

Their spongy texture soaks up the juice it is cooked in, so when you add a touch of cream it is unbelievable how the delicate texture of morels retains the juice in its wrinkled ridges.

It is complicated to find the exact cooking time a morel needs to hold onto the juice it has been cooked in while not becoming dry.

I have spent many years studying the cooking process of morels. Ducasse taught me to cook morels for 17 minutes. Escoffier had said so, Point followed, Chapel agreed and Ducasse passed it on to us. It wasn't completely wrong, but it was to my rational brain a little too rigid.

I have found over the years that morels are best cooked covered in an oven at 160°C for at least 30 minutes.

Preheat the oven to 160°C.

In a hot sauté pan melt a tablespoon of butter with the shallots and the garlic. Stir while making sure not to give any colour. Add the morels and continue stirring for 2 to 3 minutes. The morels will start releasing the little water they have. Add salt, double cream and chicken jus. Bring to the boil and remove from the heat and pour into a gratin dish.

In a bowl mix the breadcrumbs with the melting butter and toss until the breadcrumbs are well coated and look shiny. Add the chopped parsley and cover the morels with this mixture. Cover the dish with a sheet of baking parchment and cook in the pre-heated oven for 30 minutes.

Serve as soon as it is ready.

UMAMI BOMB

Parmesan & wild mushroom custard

Difficulty level: hard
Calories: 310
Preparation time: 45 minutes

I have heard everything about the fifth taste, the umami taste. My Japanese friends think they invented it. They seriously believe that they have been the only ones to use it for centuries. So now I read about the new intellectual gastronomes who rave about the deliciousness of umami and revere Japan for bringing this extra dimension to our enjoyment. Well, I can tell you that Brillat-Savarin had already managed in the nineteenth century to identify the deliciousness of food when he one day said: 'Anything brown will always taste delicious in gastronomy'.

Serves 4

- 2 tablespoons olive oil
- 100g yellow chanterelles (washed & roughly chopped)
- 100g cèpes (washed & roughly chopped)
- 40g unsalted butter
- ½ shallot (minced)
- 2 garlic cloves (minced)
- 2 thin slices pancetta (thinly sliced)
- Salt
- 1 whole egg
- 80g whipping cream
- 2 egg yolks
- 60g grated Parmesan
- 100ml whole milk
- Pepper
- 100ml chicken jus

Without going into too much depth about the process of transforming something good into something delicious, Brillat-Savarin had simply allocated a colour to something the Japanese would later claim their own under the funny name of umami. This rich mushroom custard recipe is just what you need to know about umami with a traditional Western ingredients; the umami taste is explosive!

Preheat the oven to 150°C. Pour the olive oil into a hot pan and pan-fry the mushrooms for 1 minute until they release their water. Drain and discard the cooking liquid.

Melt the butter in a thick-bottomed sauté pan. When the butter starts turning brown, add the shallots, garlic and sliced pancetta. Stir and add the mushrooms. Add salt and stir for 2 minutes making sure once again not to give any colouration (otherwise the mushrooms will taste slightly bitter).

Remove the pan from the heat and transfer the mushrooms to a plate to cool.

In a bowl, whisk together the whole egg with cream, then add the egg yolks, Parmesan and milk. Mix well while making sure that all the eggs have been combined with the other ingredients. Add the mushrooms and stir well. Taste and adjust the seasoning with salt and pepper.

Butter 4 ramekins or 4 short tumbler glasses and divide the mixture evenly among them. Place in a baking dish and pour cold water into the baking dish to reach halfway to the height of the ramekins or tumblers.

Cook in the oven for 25 minutes. Remove and allow to cool slightly while making sure that the custards are cooked by inserting a knife into one of them. If it comes out clean, it means that the custard is cooked. Just before serving, add a spoonful of warm chicken jus on top.

CÈP

Among all mushrooms, the cèp is probably the most chef friendly. It leaves plenty of room for creation. It can be served raw, cooked, as a soup and I have even seen menus with cèpes as a pudding! Not sure that would work, but you never know.

You need to get hold of fresh cèpes just after they have fruited, when they're firm and not yet infested with worms. Their nutty flavour is incomparable and they are really the essence of the woods as far as I am concerned.

Over the years, the cèp mushroom has lost a bit of its aura mainly because of tinned cèp purée and oil infused with cèpes which have been over-used and have seriously compromised the integrity of this mushroom.

I hope these simple but delicious recipes will make you realise that the cèp is still one of the greatest wild mushrooms available.

CREAM OF CÈPES

Chervil & raw cèpes

Difficulty level: medium
Calories: 180
Preparation time: 30 minutes

Serves 4

20g butter

10 small cèpes in good condition
(washed, heads & bodies separated)

40g onion (chopped thinly)

4 garlic cloves (chopped thinly)

Salt & pepper

200ml crème fraîche

500ml chicken broth

1 bunch chervil (roughly chopped)

50ml olive oil

Melt some butter in a small pan with the cèp bodies and half of the heads. Add the onion and garlic and slowly cook at low heat until the cèpes start softening and releasing their water (this should take approximately 2 to 3 minutes). Add some salt and stir again. Pour in the crème fraîche and bring to the boil. Add the chicken broth and cover. Cook for 5 minutes at low heat.

Remove the pan from the heat and pour the contents into a blender. Blend until very thin without any chunks. The consistency should be one of thick cream. Taste and rectify if it needs more salt. Do not add pepper just yet.

Divide the soup into 4 hot soup plates, sprinkle the chervil over each plate and thinly slice the remaining heads of fresh cèpes over each plate.

Add salt, black pepper and a splash of olive oil.

Serve immediately.

CÈPES & BACON

Chestnut leaves & veal jus

Difficulty level: hard
Calories: 150
Preparation time: 30 minutes

Serves 4

- 4 large chestnut leaves (washed & dried)
- 8 slices smoked streaky bacon
- 1 shallot (minced)
- 2 tablespoons unsalted butter
- 4 large fresh cèpes (lightly grated, washed & dried)
- 100ml veal jus

Preheat the oven to 160°C.

Lay the chestnut leaves flat on a clean surface. Cross 2 slices of smoked streaky bacon on top of each leaf. Place some minced shallot, a little butter and the cèp. Delicately close each cèp in its leaf and place in a buttered roasting dish.

Cook for 15 minutes. Serve them opened up in the leaf with a little veal jus. The meat jus will absorb all the deep flavours together and will create osmosis between all the ingredients.

Is there any other dish which symbolises the autumn in a more flexetarian way?

FLEXITARIAN. AM I ONE?

In a constant need to define who we are and express how we differ from one another as human beings, we have managed to fragment our race by how we feed ourselves.

The affirmation that we are what we eat will never be right in my eyes. Foods are not much more than just a collection of nutrients, especially in our current era; they do not possess a wealth of influences and connotations anymore, and we should be seriously happy with that.

It is very difficult for me to understand that some foods are worshipped in various cultures as having a special holiness, or are avoided altogether.

So with this state of mind, I found it very difficult to express what my preference really was.

Loving vegetables, while not stopping eating meat or fish, did not, until recently, have a name.

It was, to my eyes, absolutely normal to decide to indulge in plants rather than animals, just for the sake of pleasure.

Having spent many years looking at meat or fish as the centrepiece of a restaurant dish, I had been almost convinced to go against my natural inclination which was having the vegetable as the leading product in a dish, and looking at meat or fish as just flavour tools.

So when I started creating menus in my restaurant with plants as the key to a dish, people loved it straight away.

They were going crazy with what I was doing. They loved everything and they wondered how I could create so many different and delicious combinations of flavours.

'I was reincarnated as a half-baked vegetarian'

'Loving vegetables, while not stopping eating meat did not always have a name, until now'

Well, I believe that they loved it because I was cooking most of my vegetables in meat or fish stock. I would always add some grated tuna flakes or cured meat to broth, I would wrap carrots in duck skin to give them depth of flavour, I would cook stuffed tomatoes in the tray I'd used to make our beef jus, and so on.

I had never promoted my style of cooking as vegetarian and yet was niched as one of them. It took me many years to get myself the reputation of being a 'Flexitarian.'

But hold on a minute! That word is so new that even my computer doesn't recognise it.

So there I was, having managed to get rid of the Green Giant image, being reincarnated as a half-baked vegetarian.

Flexitarians are the unfinished children of vegetarians – the ones who were not quite brave enough to quit the world of animal eaters but for their good conscience have decided to carry the semi-dried Green Cross. They are the ones who can easily indulge with a Big Mac without having to repent for it.

They describe themselves as the third sex of the eating world and never feel any guilt in eating smoked salmon but they will lecture you on the benefit their diet has on the rest of the world.

No – I am not part of the new age of eating. I may be as much a flexitarian as I am a vegetarian or a pure carnivore; but why is there any need for self-classification?

SWEET & SOUR RED PICKLED ONIONS

Difficulty level: medium
Calories: 140
Preparation time: 1 hour Resting: 5 days

Onions have been cultivated for the last 5000 years. Their it's origins are in Persia, and the Egyptians were real fans. Apicius, during the Roman Empire, used onions in many recipes and the Gallic onions were his favourites. Onion is a condiment present all year long in my kitchen. It seems to me that it is one of those every-season kinds of vegetable. During winter, it brings sweetness to our stocks and soups. In spring and summer I like to add it raw to dishes. It is beautifully crunchy and sharp in taste.

Serves 4

- 400g small red onions
- 300ml white wine vinegar
- 300ml red wine vinegar
- 40g white sugar
- ½ tablespoon salt
- ¼ teaspoon cayenne pepper
- 4 garlic cloves (sliced)
- 20g ginger (peeled & sliced)
- 3 sprigs fresh thyme
- 10g fresh mint leaves
- 250ml water

In the south of France, we cook the fish *au plat* and then add thin slices of onion on top of the hot fish. When you eat it, you feel that the onion has been slightly cooked but it retains its original crunchiness and the taste is enhanced.

Start by sterilising 4 small (500ml size) jars and lids: wash them thoroughly and boil them in water.

Meanwhile, in a large cooking pot, put all the ingredients together and bring to the boil. Let them cook for 10 minutes.

Fill the jars with the onions and cover with the pickling liquid and garnishes. Make sure to leave about ½cm headroom in each jar. Place the seals and lids on each jar.

Boil them upside down in the water for 20 minutes.

Let them cool. The pickled onions will be ready to eat in 5 days.

ONION

ONION JAM

Difficulty level: easy
Calories: 30
Preparation time: 3 hours

Serves 4

- 50ml olive oil
- 200g onions (thinly sliced)
- Salt
- 40g brown sugar
- 50ml pomegranate syrup
- Pepper

In a small pan, heat the olive oil. Add the onion. Add salt, sugar, the pomegranate syrup and cover.

Cook very slowly for about 2 hours. Make sure to stir the preparation every 5 to 10 minutes. When the onions have the consistency of a compôte, remove the pan and let it cool.

Add a bit of pepper and taste. You may like to add a bit more pomegranate syrup if you feel it lacks sugar.

Serve cold.

ONION INFUSION

Difficulty level: easy
Calories: 0
Preparation time: 5 minutes

Serves 4

- 1 green onion
- Boiling water
- Garlic leaves

You have to be like me to enjoy this: passionate about the taste of onions. I have to say that I have developed this recipe after getting some sort of craving for onions.

I usually take the greenest onion available (those which make you cry as you peel!) and cut them into thick slices when they are peeled. Boil some water and pour it over the freshly cut onion.

Inhale the smell by covering your head over the bowl with a kitchen cloth. Beautiful!

NB: You can accentuate the smell by adding a few garlic leaves to the onion. And somehow I am sure that it is also good for my health!

PEAS

Before coming to the UK in 1995, I could not understand the British love for peas. It was beyond my small, closed French brain. I thought that peas eaten either mushy or over-boiled in gravy were an absolute disgrace.

How on earth could you inflict such a barbaric treatment to the refined, small, sweet and delicate little peas that I used to venerate when I was young?

I had never realised that peas had so many stages. I had been fortunate to be mostly fed with fresh, small and sweet peas by my mother. I did not know that you could actually enjoy a riper pea.

I did not know that a mature pea could bring something substantial to a dish. I now enjoy peas in many more interesting forms.

Raw, early in the season with some lemon and wasabi dressing, quickly pan-fried with baby onions in the middle of its season, and mushy pea ravioli or in soup towards the end of the season.

I also now love the hard, tough, very late peas that you can almost braise so they become little sponges for the juices they are cooked in.

EARLY-SEASON RAW PEAS

Octopus & peas in a wasabi & lemon dressing

Difficulty level: easy
Calories: 240
Preparation time: 30 minutes

Serves 4

1 teaspoon wasabi paste

1 lemon (juiced)

150ml olive oil

200g cooked octopus in oil

500g fresh peas in pods (or 200g peeled)

Salt & pepper

100g baby spinach leaves

In a small bowl, mix the wasabi paste with the lemon juice. Whisk in the olive oil until you get a light vinaigrette.

Cut the octopus into little pieces 1cm long and add them to the bowl with the vinaigrette.

Remove the peas from their shells and rinse under cold water.

Add them to the octopus and toss them together. Taste and add salt and black pepper.

Divide onto 4 plates on top of some baby spinach leaves.

You can add a splash of olive oil and lemon juice just before serving.

END-OF-SEASON MASHED PEA RAVIOLI

Difficulty level: medium
Calories: 220
Preparation time: 3 hours

Serves 4

For the stuffing

500g green peas in pods (or 200g peeled)

50ml olive oil

Salt & pepper

200ml water

1 egg

50g ricotta cheese

20g grated Parmesan

½ bunch chervil

Ravioli

1kg flour

10 eggs

3 tablespoons water

1 tablespoon white wine vinegar

Pinch salt

A little grated Parmesan

Making the stuffing

Remove the peas from their shells. In a large pan, pour a bit of olive oil and pan-fry the peas without colouration. It is important to keep the peas very green. When they are very shiny, add some salt, water and cover.

The peas should be cooked after 3 minutes: take one in your mouth and it should explode under the pressure of your tongue.

Put the peas on a plate and let them cool down a bit. Put them in a bowl and mash them with a fork or potato masher. Add the egg and mix. Add the ricotta, Parmesan, chopped chervil and mix with a wooden spoon.

When the stuffing is light but compact, adjust the seasoning with salt and pepper. Make sure you add a lot of pepper as it always accentuates the flavour of peas.

Making the ravioli

In a large vegetable bowl, place the flour, the eggs and the water. Mix with your hand until you get a dough of the same consistency all over. Add vinegar and salt and carry on stirring with your hand.

Leave in the fridge wrapped in clingfilm for a minimum of 2 hours.

Finishing the dish

Roll out the dough on a floured table. Cut some little squares (6cm x 6cm) and put a spoon of stuffing in the middle. Cover each square with another square of pasta after wetting the sides.

Cook in boiling water for 2 minutes and serve in bowls with a large splash of olive oil and some more grated Parmesan.

SAUTÉED GREEN PEAS

Button onion, sliced beef, purple basil & parsley

Difficulty level: easy
Calories: 180
Preparation time: 30 minutes

Serves 4

1 bunch purple basil

1 bunch flat-leaf parsley

200ml olive oil

150g button onions (peeled)

400g green peas (peeled & washed)

Salt & pepper

80g beef fillet (thinly sliced)

100ml balsamic vinegar

20g Parmesan shavings

Remove the leaves from both the basil and flat-leaf parsley and keep them in a bowl with the water in the coldest part of your fridge.

Put a large pan on the stove and add a bit of olive oil. When the oil starts heating, add the onion and shake the pan until the onions are shining and then add some water. Cover and cook for 6 to 8 minutes until the onions are fondant when you put a knife through them. At this moment, add the peas to the onions and toss them together. Cover and cook for an extra minute at very high heat.

Check if the peas are ready. The green peas are cooked when a slight pressure under your tongue makes them explode in your mouth. At this stage, there should not be much liquid left in the pan. Add the fresh herbs to the pan, and add salt and pepper.

Prepare 4 large plates with slices of beef covering each of them. Spoon the onion and peas over the raw beef and top them with the herbs. Pour over the olive oil and balsamic vinegar and add some Parmesan shavings.

PEPPER

It's not difficult to find a perfect red pepper these days. You just have to walk at night through the New Covent Garden market in London where most of the vegetables are bought and sold. Red peppers are there, all year round!

They are sold when asparagus are at their best and also when chestnuts are in full swing. Red pepper season is absolutely lost. I doubt that anyone remembers that summer is the best time to enjoy them.

Towards the end of June or in early July, red peppers give off a very particular green smell: a smell that tells you that peppers are sweet and juicy. It tells you that they have grown outside and have had some REAL sun. No lamps!

To choose a good pepper, you must look for the shiniest one with the tightest skin. As much as I love the smell of fresh and in-season pepper, there is one thing I can't do with them.

I can't eat them raw. They are just impossible to digest. Even the tiniest piece of red pepper will make me burp for hours and, unlike garlic or leek, the smell of the pepper burp is seriously embarrassing.

First of all, you must know that you should always remove the stem, skin and seeds of the pepper before using it in any recipe.

There are two simple ways to remove the skin. The first is to plant a fork in the red pepper and place it over an open flame. Make sure that the skin turns dark and rotate the pepper until all four faces are cracked and burnt.

The second technique is probably safer: place the pepper in a steamer for 8 to 12 minutes. Remove and throw into icy-cold water. The skin will slowly come off. You may need to use a knife to remove some of the smaller pieces of skin.

RED PEPPER

Anchovies, almond, thyme & rice

Difficulty level: medium
Calories: 237
Preparation time: 45 minutes

Serves 4

- 150ml olive oil
- 1 small onion (peeled & chopped)
- 200g long-grain rice
- Pinch salt
- 100ml dry white wine
- 4 sprigs thyme
- 300ml water
- 12 anchovy fillets (roughly chopped)
- 40g walnut (broken into small pieces)
- 60g flaked almond (slightly roasted)
- 12 small red peppers (cut to retain the top, peeled & seeded – see previous page)
- 3 large potatoes (cut into 4 slices of 1cm each)

This is one of my favourite recipes.

Preheat the oven to 160°C.

Into a hot sauté pan, add some of the olive oil and the onion. Stir on a slow heat, making the onions become shiny without giving them any colouration. Add the rice and a pinch of salt. Continue stirring on a low heat until the rice is shiny and very hot. Add the white wine and the thyme. Add the water and cover. Cook for 7 minutes on a very low heat.

Remove the rice from the heat and let it cool down for 5 minutes. In a bowl mix the anchovies, walnuts, almonds and rice together with more olive oil. Fill each red pepper with the mix and put them each on a slice of raw potato in a roasting tray. Cook in the oven for 30 minutes.

Serve on a large plate accompanied by a salad of seasoned wild rocket salad.

MASHED POTATO WITH CHERVIL & OLIVE OIL

Difficulty level: medium
Calories: 180
Preparation time: 45 minutes

Everything has been said about potatoes. We know that they are rich in potassium, vitamins B3 and C and folic acid. When I was under the weather, my mother used to grate a potato and make me drink the juice. The same beverage was prepared before an exam or a rugby match. I didn't really like it because its taste was very bland and the texture was strange. Like sucking a cat's tongue! I preferred the potato purée she used to make with olive oil and chervil. My mother's favourite potato was the Bintje: perfectly yellow, moist and easily breakable once cooked.

Serves 4

- 2 large Bintje potatoes (or very pale jacket potatoes)
- 2 tablespoons sea salt
- 250ml olive oil
- ½ basil bunch (roughly chopped)
- Salt & pepper
- 2 chervil bunches (roughly chopped)
- 100ml chicken jus
- 40g grated Parmesan

Wash the potatoes under cold water, making sure to remove any dirt. Put them in a large pot, fully covered with water. Add the sea salt and cook at a slow simmer for about 20 minutes.

Check from time to time with a small knife to see if the potatoes are cooked. The potato is cooked when there is no resistance to the knife.

Remove the potatoes from the water and peel them while very hot.

Put them back in the pot with a little water and salt.

Start smashing them with a fork while pouring in some olive oil. When the potatoes are puréed, add some more oil and carry on smashing with a fork. Add the chopped basil and ground pepper.

Taste and rectify by adding some more salt or pepper.

Don't be afraid to put a lot of chervil in – it will taste even better.

Serve it as it is or add a splash of chicken jus and a sprinkling of grated parmesan if you wish to.

JERSEY NEW POTATOES

Cooked in brown butter with Parmesan & flat-leaf parsley

Difficulty level: easy
Calories: 200
Preparation time: 30 minutes5

Serves 4

100g butter

24 small Jersey Royal potatoes

Salt

400ml chicken broth

50g grated Parmesan

20g Japanese breadcrumbs (because they are very light; you can also use ordinary ones)

½ flat-leaf parsley bunch

Preheat the oven to 220°C.

Into a thick-bottomed pan, put a large spoonful of butter. Heat until the butter turns brown, then add the potatoes. Stir and add salt. The potatoes have to be coloured uniformly. Add the chicken broth and put in the oven for 15 minutes.

Check that the potatoes are perfectly cooked all the way by slightly pressing on their skins.

Remove the pan from the oven and put the potatoes in a serving dish. Reduce the juice left in the pan until it gets thicker and pour over the potatoes with some grated parmesan, Japanese breadcrumbs and flat-leaf parsley.

You can serve this dish with a simple lettuce salad.

When comes the autumn, so comes the pumpkin! The sight of a pumpkin reminds me that summer is over and autumn is here. I like pumpkin. Firstly, I like its shape. I like its enormity. When I was young, I remember going to the vegetable market with my mother. I was horrified by the sight of this giant 'melon'. On top of that, I hated the sight of its inside: full of scary orange hair. I wouldn't like to be near it. But since then, I have discovered its taste and texture, the pumpkin has become a great friend.

The first time I had to cook a pumpkin was when I was in Monte Carlo. They do the most fantastic pumpkin risotto: very creamy, shiny and rich. I realised that pumpkin was a top ingredient. Since then, I have always heavily featured pumpkin during the autumn months.

The pumpkin always stands next to the best ingredients available on the menu. It is often a starter on its own: polenta pumpkin with chicken jus or roasted with baby red chard and bergamot dressing.

In main courses it becomes the best partner for venison and truffle, or as a cream with steamed John Dory. It can also be a fantastic pudding – see the pumpkin cake I used to prepare while in San Francisco for Halloween.

Pumpkin seeds are also great. When roasted they are better than any other roasted seeds. The Greeks and Romans used to make a body lotion out of them. They used it for its anti-ageing properties as well as its nourishing qualities.

Pumpkin is the Autumn King.

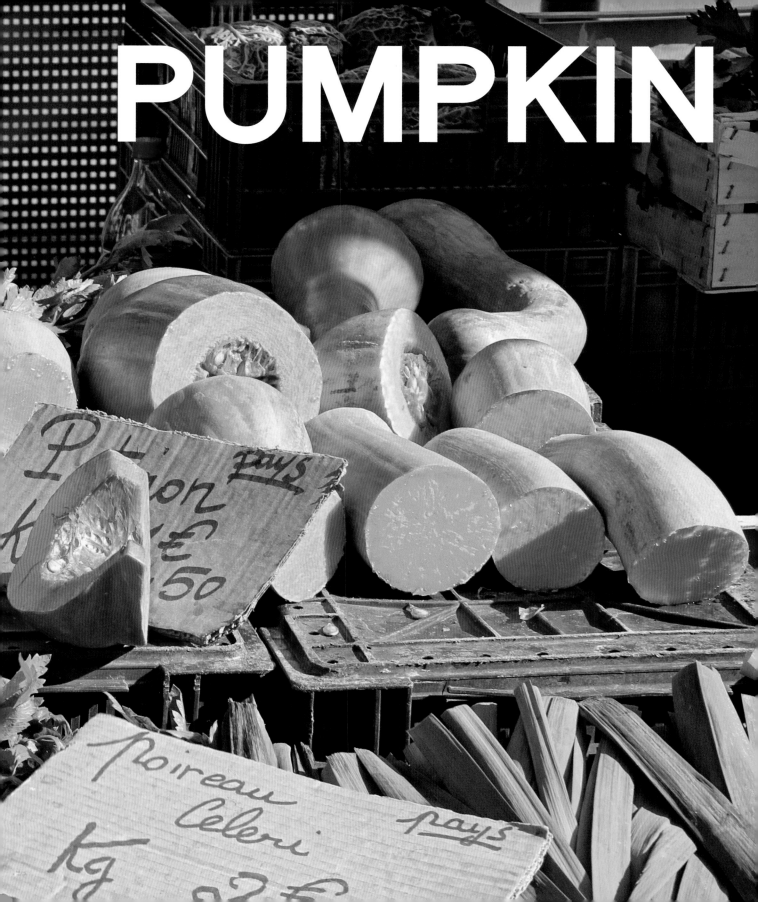

PUMPKIN

PUMPKIN & CUMIN SOUP

Ricotta gnocchi & Parmesan

Difficulty level: medium
Calories: 140
Preparation time: 1 hour

Serves 4

Pumpkin Soup

500g pumpkin

200ml olive oil

100ml fat-free liquid cream (it suprisingly cooks without splitting. The best is available from Co-op)

200ml chicken broth

Salt

White pepper

Ricotta gnocchi

150g fresh ricotta cheese

1 tablespoon cornflour

1 egg

20g grated Parmesan

Salt

White pepper

To Serve

Grated Parmesan

1 teaspoon ground cumin

Making the pumpkin cream

Preheat the oven to 220°C.

Cut the pumpkin carefully into very big chunks with the skin on. Place the pumpkin chunks into a pre-oiled roasting tray with salt. Do not add any liquid as the pumpkin will release its water under the heat of the oven. Put the tray in the oven for 15 minutes. The pumpkin should have softened with a pale golden-brown skin over the flesh. Let the pumpkin cool down. Spoon the flesh out and put it in a blender. Blend until the purée looks free of any lumps.

Boil the cream and the chicken broth together with a pinch of salt and some white pepper. When it boils, add it to the pumpkin pulp. Taste, rectify the seasoning if needed and put to one side.

Making the ricotta gnocchi

In the bowl of the blender, put the ricotta, cornflour, egg, Parmesan, salt and pepper. Make sure all of the ingredients are well mixed together.

Transfer to a small bowl and keep in the fridge for 4 hours or in the freezer for 30 minutes.

Boil the water with a pinch of salt and keep it at a simmer. Take a spoon of the gnocchi mix and plunge it directly into the boiling water. The heat and water will lift the mix from the spoon. Let them boil for 2 minutes and delicately remove them before putting them onto an oiled plate.

Reheat the soup. Place the gnocchi into each plate sprinkled with a little Parmesan. Pour the soup into the plate and add a pinch of cumin on the side.

PUMPKIN RISOTTO

Difficulty level: hard
Calories: 300
Preparation time: 1 hour

Serves 4

150ml olive oil

80g onion

250g Italian risotto rice

Salt

100ml white wine

1 litre hot chicken stock

400g pumpkin

40g mascarpone

30g unsalted butter

120g grated Parmesan

50ml whipped cream

Pepper

50ml beef jus

Thinly chop the onion and heat it in a pan with 25ml olive oil until it becomes translucent.

Add the rice and a pinch of salt and warm the rice up to the point that you cannot touch it.

Stir without stopping and pour over the white wine. Start pouring in the chicken stock slowly for 5 minutes. The rice has to swim all the time in the same amount of liquid at very slow simmer. After 5 minutes, drain the rice and spread it thinly on a tray in order to make it cool down quicker. Make sure to keep the cooking juice from the rice. It is indispensable when you finish cooking the risotto later.

Peel the pumpkin with a very sharp knife. Mind your fingers while peeling the pumpkin. You need to concentrate on your movement.

Make sure to have removed all of the 'hair' left in the pumpkin. Pour some olive oil in a pan and put in the pumpkin, thickly chopped. Stir without giving any colouration, add some salt, cover and cook at a low heat. You do not need to add water since the pumpkin is very moist. After 6 to 7 minutes the pumpkin should be cooked. Retain 12 small pieces of pumpkin for serving. Remove the cover and stir it in order to dry it out slightly.

Blend the pumpkin in a food processor and put the purée to one side.

Put the rice in a pan with the pumpkin purée and 500ml of rice jus. Bring to the boil and then start to incorporate the ingredients one after the other, making sure that it stays simmering.

Firstly, add a spoon of mascarpone, then the butter, Parmesan (two spoonfuls), the remaining olive oil, whipped cream, salt and pepper. Serve immediately.

The risotto has to be 'wavy'- not hard and not soft, just in between. It is actually the olive oil added at the end that will make the difference. It will make your risotto stay creamy!

Divide the risotto into 4 soup plates, topped with the retained pieces of pumpkin, and pour beef jus around. Finish with a sprinkle of Parmesan.

PUMPKIN & ORANGE BLOSSOM CAKE

Difficulty level: medium
Calories: 250
Preparation time: 2 hours

Serves 6

- 600g pumpkin (peeled)
- 110g butter
- 200ml milk
- 75g sugar
- 6 tablespoons cornflour
- 1 teaspoon orange blossom water
- Salt
- 3 eggs
- 250g ground almonds

Cut the pumpkin into small squares, cover and cook them with 50g of butter for 20 minutes.

Transfer to a blender and purée. Add the milk, sugar and 60g butter.

Mix well, move to a saucepan and bring to boiling point. Dissolve the cornflour in water, add to the pan and cook for a further 2 minutes.

Remove from the heat and cool. Add the blossom water and salt.

Separate the yolks and the whites from the eggs. Add the three yolks to the pumpkin preparation one after the other. Whisk the whites until hard and incorporate them slowly. Add the ground almonds delicately. Cook for 45 minutes in a buttered cake mould (20cm diameter) at 175°C.

If you want to do as I have done, fill up 6 Oto silicone moulds, pictured. You can find out where to buy them in the special equipment section on page 374–375.

Serve warm with fresh cream.

GARDEN

SALAD

When picked young, lettuce has some beautiful fresh flavours and smells like fresh grass. It is also very refreshing and its light crunchiness is subtle in the mouth.

Lettuce is very easy to grow in the garden. It does not require special soil or a lot of space. In the UK, for example, there are many companies selling garden salad seeds.

Growing your own salad is something very special and you will feel a lot healthier. The best way to eat garden leaves is in salad. You can cook winter lettuce, but if possible always eat it raw.

GARDEN SALAD

CRAQUANTE D'AVIGNON (CRUNCHY FROM AVIGNON)

I love this one. This is the queen of the Avignon vegetable market. It is a fat lettuce with thick leaves and a very crunchy stalk. This salad can really retain its crunchiness, even if the dressing has been covering its leaves for a while. The leaves are a little peppery and because of their fatness, they tend to get stuck between the teeth sometimes. Watch out after consuming.

CUTTING LETTUCE FAMILY: LOLLO BIONDO

The famous Lollo is now everywhere, actually bit too everywhere for my liking! It tends to wilt very quickly under the power of vinegar. I would suggest eating the Lollo with a simple dressing made of a very fruity and young olive oil, and salt and pepper only.

GREEN OAKLEAF

Deeply indented green leaves, with slight brownish edges. This is my sandwich salad. It always works and rarely turns mushy under the weight and fattiness of mayonnaise.

WILD ROCKET *(Pictured)*

I was first introduced to wild rocket in Alain Ducasse's kitchen. There were always two kinds of rocket: bouquet (as in bunched) and wild. When I tasted the bitter green and peppery leaves for the first time, I really wondered what this salad was doing in a 3-Michelin-star kitchen.

Why would people pay a fortune for this bitter extravaganza? Since then I have learned to appreciate the power of the bitter, peppery rush you get as soon as you have swallowed one leaf. It is an acquired taste.

SALAD DRESSINGS

Difficulty level: easy

Garden salad is and will forever be a part of my daily meal. Even though it has long been proven to be absolutely useless for your body and your general well-being, I still find salad inspiring. Depending on my mood, season or even the kind of dressing, I would use a different kind: curly, bitter, very pale, bright and full of chlorophyll, or just plain crunchy for the pleasure of chewing. I love the diversity: either wild or cultivated, lettuce has always been in my kitchen.

LEMON & MUSTARD DRESSING

Calories : 95
Preparation time: 10 minutes

Serves 4

2 frisée lettuce

2 tablespoons Dijon mustard

2 lemons (juice)

200ml olive oil

4 tablespoons red wine vinegar

Salt & pepper

My mother made sure that we ate a decent amount of fresh salad on a daily basis. She used to prepare classic grain mustard vinaigrette to go with it. My Uncle Henry liked lemon vinaigrette. Extremely acidic and always paired with plenty of black pepper. It took me many years to enjoy it. I am now absolutely addicted to this lemon dressing. His favourite salad to go with this acidic dressing was the frisée (or oak leaves) with tough stems and bitter yellow curly leaves.

Clean the frisée by removing all of its green leaves. Wash under cold water and drain until dry. Whisk the mustard and lemon juice together. When you start to get a thick paste, slowly add the olive oil, making sure that it doesn't split.

Add the red wine vinegar and add the salt and pepper. Toss the salad in the bowl and serve.

BLACK TRUFFLE & CHICKEN JUS DRESSING

Calories: 319
Preparation time: 30 minutes

Serves 4

1 hard-boiled egg

1 teaspoon Amora mustard

1 tablespoon fresh black truffle (chopped)

150ml virgin olive oil

Salt & pepper

150ml truffle oil

150ml chicken jus

2 Cos lettuce

Cos or Romaine are the best. Crunchy light-green leaves, and when coated in a truffle vinaigrette with chicken jus it is absolute heaven.

In a large salad bowl, break up the hard-boiled egg with a fork until you get it to a mushy texture. Add the Amora mustard and the chopped black truffle. Pour in the olive oil. Add the salt, pepper and truffle oil.

Reheat the chicken jus.

Divide the salad into 4 large plates. Pour the dressing over the salad and finish with a spoon of chicken jus on each plate.

GREEN SALAD

PERELLA RED, GRAIN MUSTARD DRESSING

Serves 4

Difficulty level: easy
Calories: 70
Preparation time: 10 minutes

1 egg yolk

3 tablespoons grain mustard

150ml olive oil

3 tablespoons white wine vinegar

Salt & pepper

2 red perella

When you choose a green salad, make sure that the leaves are thin, smooth and crunchy. The salad should be heavy and spotless. The sooner you eat it, the better it is when it comes to salad. The one which I come across very often is perella red: it tastes really sweet and is always delicious when tossed with grain mustard dressing.

In a salad bowl, whisk the egg yolk slowly with the grain mustard. When it starts looking like a brownish paste, slowly pour in the olive oil. Whisk in the white wine vinegar, salt and pepper. Toss with the perella and serve.

BRAISED LETTUCE, BEEF JUS & GOLDEN CROUTONS

Difficulty level: hard
Calories: 190
Preparation time: 30 minutes

Serves 4

3 round lettuce

20g butter

40g onion (chopped)

2 garlic cloves (chopped)

100g carrot (chopped)

100g button mushrooms (chopped)

Pinch salt

1 litre chicken stock

150ml beef jus

2 slices white bread (cut into small cubes)

50ml olive oil

Wash the lettuce by removing one layer of the outside leaves. Remove 2 unstained leaves on each lettuce head. Boil them for 5 seconds in order to stabilise their colour. We will use them to wrap the braised lettuce at the end.

Boil the whole heads of lettuce in water for 1 minute and refresh them in cold water (the heads of lettuce will have seriously reduced in size).

In a large pan, slowly heat the butter and when it starts foaming, throw in the onion, garlic, carrot and mushroom. Add salt and stir at a low heat. Lay the lettuce on top and cover with chicken stock. Cover with a lid and slowly cook for 15 minutes. Remove the lid and let the liquid evaporate.

Wrap each lettuce head (with a spoonful of vegetable garnish) in 2 quickly boiled lettuce leaves. Lay them on an oiled serving tray and drizzle some warm beef jus over.

Serve with golden brown cubes of white bread pan-fried in olive oil.

Salsify is a root vegetable commonly found at farmers' markets from November until February. It is almost impossible to find it in a supermarket. We may be able to find it in a tin but never fresh.

The reason is that people do not know how to use it. It is difficult to peel and takes a long time to prepare.

I also think that a big problem stems from the fact that most chefs and cookery books tell you to boil salsify in water in order to cook it. So it never tastes really memorable.

I mean that you should never boil a root, but always simmer it in water and butter. It is the only way to cook it: it will be moist, tender and full of flavour.

Another annoying thing is that those cookery books tell you to rub it with lemon once peeled to stop it turning black. As with the artichoke, it is absolute nonsense to use lemon since you want to retain the original taste, and that has nothing to do with lemon.

Put them in icy water and cook them just after peeling.

SALSIFY

FONDANT SALSIFY

FONDANT SALSIFY & MARROW GRATIN

Serves 4

Difficulty level: medium
Calories: 320
Preparation time: 1 hour

400g salsify

200g butter

1200ml water

Salt

8 veal marrows (boiled in salted water for 3 minutes & refreshed)

Pepper

Grated Parmesan

100ml beef jus

Wash and peel the salsify and put in icy water.

In a large thick-bottomed pan, put the butter, salsify and water. Add some salt, cover and cook for 20 minutes. After 15 minutes, start checking how the salsify are by testing their resistance with a knife. If there is still resistance, it means that the salsify is not completely cooked. You need to be careful, as once the salsify is ready, it turns to mush very quickly.

Remove the salsify one by one and lay them in a baking tray. Reduce the cooking juice until it gets quite thick, and pour over the salsify in the baking tray.

Preheat the oven to 180°C. Slice the marrow and place on top of the salsify. Add some pepper, sprinkle over some Parmesan and add the beef jus. Bake in the oven for 10 minutes and serve.

FONDANT SALSIFY & CRAYFISH

Serves 6

Difficulty level: hard
Calories: 310
Preparation time: 1 hour 30 minutes

300g salsify

200g butter

1200ml water

Salt & pepper

100ml prawn jus

50ml single cream

20 crayfish (cooked for 5 minutes in salted boiling water & peeled)

½ bunch flat-leaf parsley (roughly chopped)

½ bunch coriander (roughly chopped)

Cook the salsify as in the previous recipe.

Into a small pan, pour the prawn jus and the single cream. Boil them together and add the salsify and crayfish. Cover and slowly cook for 3 minutes.

Remove the cover and finish by tossing them together with a bit of pepper.

Plate the salsify and crayfish together and sprinkle with parsley and coriander.

Pour the remaining jus around and serve.

TOMATO

The smell of a raw tomato is something that you will never forget. Every time I come across tomatoes I have to smell them. Most importantly, I smell their stalks. It reminds me of where I grew up, Avignon, where tomato is used in almost every dish.

When I was young, from March until October I would eat tomatoes in all their various forms for lunch and dinner – they would be served in soup, salad, stuffed, as a starter, a main course and even as a pudding.

Tomatoes are good for me, and I need them.

Apparently, eating large quantities can interfere with calcium absorption, but I have never felt anything wrong despite eating them in very large quantities.

A tomato is rich in magnesium, phosphorus, folic acid and vitamin C. It is also a good antiseptic and reduces liver infection.

Choosing a good tomato can be tricky – especially in the UK where most tomatoes are already pre-packaged when you buy them. A good one should be heavy in hand, smell slightly green and its skin should be tight and spotless.

My favourite kind is the 'roma', which is available from July until October everywhere in Northern Europe. It is actually the very best variety for a fresh tomato salad.

TOMATO

FRESH TOMATO PULP

Serves 4

Difficulty level: easy
Calories: 40
Preparation time: 4 hours

- 1kg tomatoes
- 1 bunch fresh tarragon
- 4 tablespoons Xeres vinegar
- Salt & pepper
- 1 tablespoon brown sugar
- 100ml olive oil

Remove the skin of the tomatoes after immersing them for 10 seconds in boiling water.

Chop the tomatoes very thinly until they become almost liquid.

Pass them through a muslin cloth and squeeze. Drain the pulp for 3 hours until it is almost completely dry.

Meanwhile, wash and dry the tarragon leaves. Chop them and keep them to one side.

Put the drained pulp in a bowl and add a splash of the Xeres vinegar, salt, pepper, sugar, olive oil and tarragon. Mix the sauce with a fork and serve it at room temperature.

Delicious with toasted slices of baguette.

CONFIT TOMATO

Serves 6

Difficulty level: medium
Calories: 50
Preparation time: 1½ hours

- 1kg tomatoes
- 4 tablespoons honey
- Salt & pepper
- ½ bunch fresh thyme
- 4 garlic cloves
- 200ml olive oil

Preheat the oven to 120°C.

Remove the skins of the tomatoes as above. Cut the tomatoes into quarters. Remove their pulp, making sure not to leave any seeds.

Dry them individually with a kitchen cloth.

Put them on a baking tray. Brush them on both sides with a mixture made of honey, salt, pepper, fresh thyme, crushed garlic and olive oil.

Then put them in the oven with the door slightly open for 1 hour.

TOMATO

TOMATO JAM

Serves 4

Difficulty level: easy
Calories: 80
Preparation time: 4 hours

1kg late-season tomatoes

50g unsalted butter

3 tablespoons brown sugar

50g pickled ginger (thinly chopped)

1 lemon (juiced)

300ml water

Thickly chop the last tomatoes of the season and put aside.

In a large hot pan, brown the butter, then throw in the tomatoes and stir vigorously for 3 minutes. Then add the brown sugar and stir again.

Add the pickled ginger, the lemon juice and a good amount of water.

Cook on a low heat for 3 hours. When the water has evaporated from the tomatoes and it looks like a jam, remove the pan and let it cool.

Serve cold with fresh oysters, toasted bread or grilled aubergine, for example.

MUSTARD & TOMATO FEUILLETÉ

Difficulty level: medium
Calories: 220
Preparation time: 45 minutes

Serves 6

500g tomatoes

1 good-quality puff pastry roll

60g Dijon mustard

40g grated Parmesan

Fresh thyme

Black pepper

My mother probably cut out this recipe from the food section of *Cosmopolitan* in the summer of 1978 – it featured on the front of our fridge for years afterwards. It is the most simple and delicious tomato recipe that has ever been invented.

Preheat the oven to 180°C.

Remove the peduncle of each tomato. Cut them into slices ½cm thick.

Roll out the puff pastry and spread the mustard generously. Place the tomatoes over it and sprinkle over the Parmesan, fresh thyme and pepper.

Cook in the hot oven for 12 minutes, then finish cooking the tart for another 3 minutes with the oven door slightly open so the humidity can evaporate.

Add a splash of olive oil just before serving.

TRUFFLE

One may think that because of its rarity and high cost black truffle is a very special ingredient. Black truffle is no caviar. Black truffle is an aroma, a penetrating aroma. There is no folklore or anything mystical about it, but it is truly a special ingredient.

What makes this ingredient so special is the fact that you can't really learn how to use it. It takes years of practice and experimentation to start recognising its qualities and using it judiciously.

You can buy black truffle in a tin, in purée, infused in oil and of course fresh. You can infuse it, cook it, add it to a mixture but over the years, I have found that raw truffle is really the best.

It doesn't usually get interfered with by other ingredients and always brings a depth of aroma that complements the flavour of what it is mixed with.

So, if you are still convinced that truffle is merely an expensive oddity, try the simple black truffle polenta.

SUMMER TRUFFLE RISOTTO

Difficulty level: hard
Calories: 345
Preparation time: 30 minutes

Serves 4

½ onion

250g Carnaroli rice

250ml olive oil

50ml white wine

500ml chicken broth

50g butter

50g grated Parmesan

80g mascarpone

2 tablespoons whipped cream

50ml truffle oil

Salt & white pepper

100ml chicken jus

40g summer truffle

Chop the onion, fry it with the rice in olive oil without colouration, then add the white wine and allow to evaporate until almost dry. Slowly add the chicken broth and cook for 14 minutes while stirring regularly.

Add the butter little by little, some of the Parmesan, mascarpone and a little olive oil. Make sure the consistency is unctuous. If too hard, add a spoonful of whisked whipped cream. Finish with truffle oil.

Taste to adjust the seasoning.

Divide the risotto between 4 soup plates and pour over some warmed chicken jus. Finish by covering the risotto with some thinly sliced black truffle.

BLACK TRUFFLE POLENTA

Difficulty level: medium
Calories: 235
Preparation time: 40 minutes

Serves 4

100ml olive oil

50g celery (cut into small cubes)

50g pumpkin (peeled & cut into small cubes)

120g coarse cornmeal polenta

100ml dry white wine

1 litre chicken broth

30g mascarpone

2 Savoy cabbage leaves (boiled for 2 minutes and cut into small cubes)

40g grated Parmesan

Salt & pepper

20g black Perigord truffle

Into a large pot on a high heat add 1 tablespoon of olive oil until hot. Add in the celery and pumpkin and stir, making sure not to give any colouration. Add the polenta and carry on stirring on a low heat. Add the white wine and reduce until almost dry.

Add the chicken broth gradually, and slowly and constantly stir using the handle of a wooden spoon. It helps break down polenta.

Cook for another 6 minutes until the polenta starts thickening and is not 'swimming' any more in the broth. Add the mascarpone and carry on cooking at a low heat. Add the Savoy cabbage and the Parmesan. Finish by adding the remaining olive oil. By then the mixture should have a not-too-thick creamy texture.

Add the salt and pepper and divide the polenta between 4 soup plates. Slice the fresh truffle over each plate and serve immediately.

LATE-SUMMER TRUFFLE

Simmered autumn vegetables

Difficulty level: hard
Calories: 110
Preparation time: 45 minutes

Serves 4

- 30g unsalted butter
- 80g celeriac (diced)
- 80g carrot (diced)
- Salt & pepper
- 60g parsnip (diced)
- 60g leek (diced)
- 60g white potato (diced)
- 1 fresh summer truffle (around 25/30g)
- 100ml dry white wine
- 250ml chicken broth

Melt the butter and when it starts foaming, add the celeriac and carrot. Add a pinch of salt and stir on a very low heat. After 2 minutes, add the parsnip, leek and potatoes. Stir for another 2 minutes while making sure that nothing sticks to the bottom of the pan. Add another small pinch of salt.

Add 5g of chopped black truffle and pour in the white wine. Reduce the white wine until it is almost dry and add the chicken broth. Bring to a simmer and cover. Cook for 7 minutes.

Check every 2 to 3 minutes to ensure that the heat is not excessive.

Once the vegetables are fondant but not mushy, remove them from the heat and spoon them out into soup plates.

Add a little pepper to each plate and thinly slice the summer truffle over. Eat straight away.

TURNIP

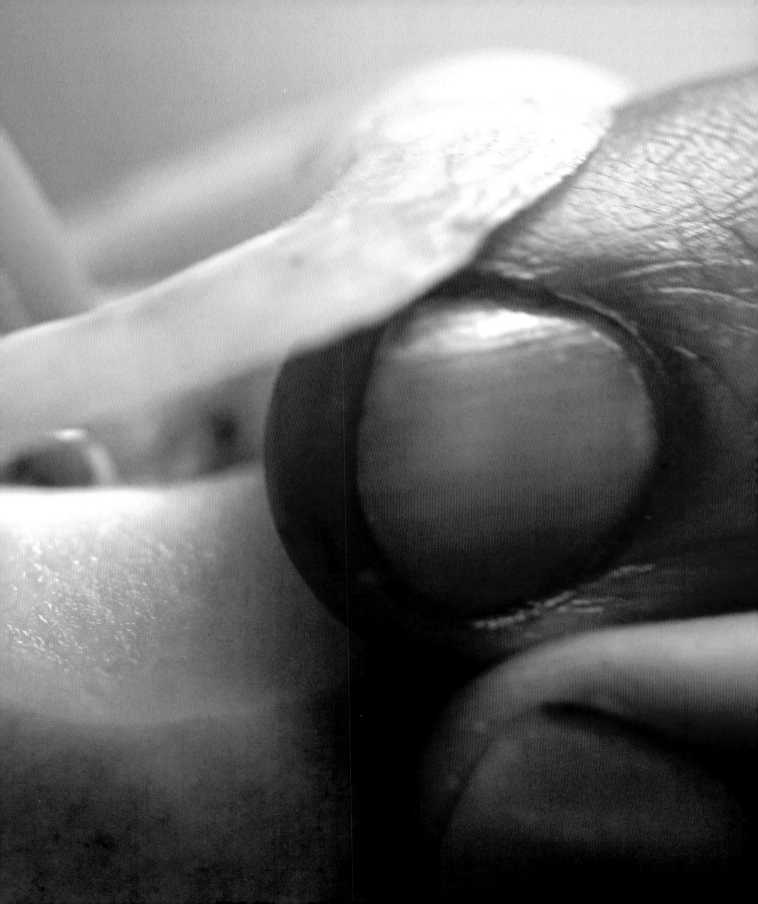

TURNIPS APICIUS

Difficulty level: hard
Calories: 180
Preparation time: 45 minutes

Being called a turnip is slightly pejorative and isn't very flattering.

It seems rather unfair that such a beautiful vegetable is used to describe someone lacking in character. This dish will make you proud when you are next called a turnip.

Serves 4

- 2 bunches small round turnips (around 30)
- 50ml olive oil
- Salt
- 10g sugar
- 1 litre chicken broth
- 12 fresh dates (stones removed)
- 50g butter
- 3 Granny Smith apples

Apicius mix

- 2 tablespoons honey
- 10g coriander seeds
- 10g fennel seeds
- 10g black pepper
- 10g cumin seeds
- 20ml dry white wine
- 2 mint leaves

Separate the turnips from their stems, retaining 2cm attached.

Twice peel each turnip and keep them in cold water. Keep in the fridge for 30 minutes so they get very cold.

Start preparing the apicius mix by heating up the honey, coriander seeds, fennel seeds, black pepper and cumin seeds together in a pan on a very low heat. When the seeds start caramelising, add the white wine and mint leaves.

Let it simmer slowly until it starts thickening. Make sure to brush the side of the pan from time to time so it doesn't burn.

When the apicius mix starts looking like a thick honey, remove from the heat and keep at room temperature.

Pour some olive oil into a large pan on high heat. When the oil starts smoking, add the turnips and stir for 20 seconds. Add salt and sugar. Add the chicken broth and cover. It should take 5 minutes for the turnips to reach a fondant texture.

Add the dates to the turnips and cook for another 3 minutes. Add two spoonfuls of the apicius mix and let the liquid evaporate.

Remove the pan when the turnips and dates start caramelising. Lay them on a plate, alternating the dates and turnips. Put the pan back on a high heat and add another spoonful of apicius mix together with the butter. The butter will create a sauce with the apicius mix.

Pour this sauce over the turnips and dates and add some very thinly sliced Granny Smith apples.

BITTER SLICES OF RAW TURNIP
Tuna & wasabi mayonnaise

Difficulty level: medium
Calories: 150
Preparation time: 30 minutes

This simple salad is all about texture. The crunchy, bitter slices of tiny turnips bring texture to a soft and creamy slice of fatty tuna. The whole thing comes together in the rich wasabi mayonnaise that glues everything together. The turnip leaves bring a bit of refreshment to the combination without taking over the original texture and flavour. A simple, well constructed and seriously impressive salad.

Serves 4

- 100g small turnips (with their leaves)
- 1 egg yolk
- 1 tablespoon sweet soy sauce
- 1 teaspoon wasabi
- 200ml sunflower oil
- Salt
- 2 limes (juiced)
- White pepper
- 200g toro (fatty) tuna loin (trimmed and then frozen)

Remove the greenest turnip leaves and wash them under cold water. Dry them with a kitchen cloth and store them in the fridge.

Wash and peel the turnips. Keep them in icy water. Slice them very thinly with a Japanese mandolin (or a very sharp knife if you haven't got one) and put them in ice. They will become crunchier.

In a bowl, whisk the egg yolk and soy sauce with the wasabi and slowly add the sunflower oil. Carry on whisking until it becomes the texture of a liquid mayonnaise. Add a pinch of salt, the juice of one lime and some white pepper.

Remove the tuna from the freezer and cut some thin slices with a long knife.

In a bowl, season the crunchy slices of turnips with the mayonnaise.

On 4 large plates, alternate the slices of toro tuna with the slices of turnips and the fresh turnip leaves. Finish by pouring the juice of the other lime with some salt and pepper.

BECOMING A HAIRDRESSER

It is common knowledge that kitchens are not reknowned for refined and distinguished conversation. It is usually somewhere that pretty much everyone swears, shouts, abuses and sometimes hits one another.

Having spent too many years working in kitchens, I could write an entire book about capricious, inflated, egocentric chefs who commonly abuse their staff.

So when I reached the highlight of my apprenticeship by working in a 3-Michelin-star kitchen, I knew that I would have to suffer many insults . . . I was ready for that. What I wasn't ready for was a question my head chef would ask me, day in day out, for over two years: Why don't you become a hairdresser?

From the moment I entered the kitchen until the moment I left at night, I was subjected to the most terrible harassment one can imagine. He would constantly question my desire to become a chef. And the question wasn't naive at all. Being a hairdresser is the complete opposite of the macho image a chef has to have.

So glad was I at not having followed his cheap career advice that I married a hairdresser!

FRUITS

Like a new partner, a fruit needs to be touched to tell you how good it is going to be. Fruit is an obsession for me. I am fascinated by its diversity and how it impacts on one's life. Everyone has a favourite fruit, and you can always tell a lot about someone by the fruit he or she prefers. Tell me what fruit you love and I will tell you who you are.

My Uncle Henry, who pretty much brought me up, was the king of fruit at home. Unsurprising, since he was chief trader for the Avignon fruit market! He lived his life around fruit, its qualities and its prices.

He loved talking about them, talking to them and he naturally loved eating them. He was so much into his fruit that he slowly developed fruit shapes in his body. His face was as round as a tangerine, his arms were like two bananas, his legs were as strong as pineapples and his chest was like a big grapefruit.

He respected fruit and understood it like nobody else. He would also always try to find a good excuse when a fruit was not so good: maybe the weather, maybe the producer, but never the fruit itself. As far as he was concerned, fruit was always perfect. No matter its shape or its colour.

I believed every word he said, until I started travelling!

When I first arrived in California in 1995, I was taken to Stanford shopping centre where I was told that I could find the very best seasonal fruits. We were there in mid-December and I imagined I would find the same sort of fruit I could find in any south-of-France market since the weather was quite similar – the softest persimmon, the shiniest dates, the first oranges of the season, and the sharpest lemons.

In fact, I found myself looking at beautifully arranged rows of imported cherries, uniform raspberries, plenty of exotic fruit and for each fruit a picture of the farmer smiling happily in the middle of his field. What the hell, I thought. Fruit was no longer a marker of the season we were in. I can't describe the precise feeling I had on that December day. Fruit was lost, and I was lost.

(cont.)

Then I saw a massive strawberry. I had been cheated, the fruit had been cheated, and I was supposed to find amazing the sight of a 2kg bloated strawberry. Even more annoying was being told that I could keep it for at least 3 weeks and could feed up to 10 adults with it.

Suddenly fruit had lost their promise.

I decided to venture out to find some persimmon to purchase. Sadly they had been wrapped in a packet of two and below the cheesy picture of the smiling farmer was written in capital letters:

DO NOT TOUCH THE FRUIT.

What? Was I supposed to imagine what they would taste like in my mouth without feeling their skin under my fingers? Exactly so!

It became very stressful. I had spent more than twenty years developing my understanding of fruit by touching it, smelling it and pressing it before putting it in my mouth and here I was trying to spot the one with the darkest colour and the shiniest skin. I picked up a packet of two – one of them was great, the other one was too hard and not ready to be eaten.

Silly me, I should have known; I should have recognised the perfect one, the one next to this one maybe. But I couldn't: my hands, which are supposed to help me choose, had to stay away from the fruit.

It is like going to a museum and being asked not to touch the art. Frustrating! I don't want to be frustrated, I want to use my hands. I want to use all of my senses.

From that day, I promised myself that I would never buy any fruit I hadn't touched or smelled beforehand.

APPLE

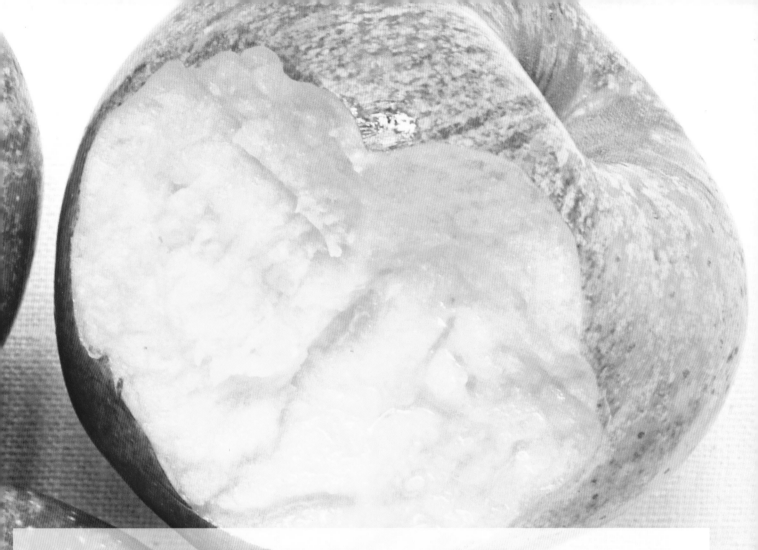

An apple a day keeps the doctor away. We have all been told this.

Actually, it is not one but three a day that we should be eating. Three apples a day for 45 days is said to reduce your cholesterol by between 10% to 40% apparently. In order to achieve this you have to eat the apple unpeeled otherwise it will take a little bit longer to work. I should actually be writing about the pectin instead of the apple. Pectin is very good for slowing the process of absorbing sugar into the blood. It protects our pancreas while reducing our intake of insulin.

We all need to eat apples; best will be to take them at the beginning of each meal. It will help your system digest the sugar and the grease more easily.

There are many kinds of apples available and it is sometimes quite hard to find the one that is going to work best with what you are going to make. The following pages will indicate the guidelines I follow.

APPLE

DEEP-FRIED: SWEET APPLE TEMPURA

Serves 4

Difficulty level: medium
Calories: 280
Preparation time: 45 minutes

100g tempura mix (you can find this in Japanese supermarkets)

100ml very cold water

1kg Melrose apples

500ml sunflower oil

Icing sugar

In a bowl, mix the tempura powder with the water. Whisk until you get a thin creamy paste free of any lumps.

Peel and core the apples. Cut them into any shape as long as they are all of the same thickness of around 1cm.

Heat some sunflower oil to 200°C (drop a touch of tempura mix into the oil when you feel it is hot enough. If the tempura sets and start frying, your oil is ready).

Coat the apple in the tempura mix and cook in the hot oil, turning the pieces of apple over after 2 minutes. Remove them from the hot oil and drain them on a cloth. Sprinkle on some icing sugar and serve.

OVEN-ROASTED: POMEGRANATE ROASTED APPLE

Serves 4

Difficulty level: medium
Calories: 324
Preparation time: 30 minutes

8 Golden Delicious apples

60g butter (cut into small cubes)

8 tablespoons honey

8 tablespoons pomegranate syrup

2 fresh pomegranate (seeds)

Preheat the oven to 180°C. Clean the apples but do not peel. Core and remove all of its seeds.

Lay the apples in a buttered roasting dish. Put a spoonful of butter in the middle of each apple, add a spoonful of honey, a spoonful of pomegranate syrup and some pomegranate seeds.

Put into the oven for 10 minutes at 180°C. Serve immediately.

APPLE

BAKED

Difficulty level: easy
Calories: 80
Preparation time: 1 hour 30 minutes Marinating: 12 hours

Serves 4

2 oranges (juiced)

½ glass Alsatian wine (preferably Riesling)

2 tablespoons brown sugar

1 teaspoon cinnamon

1 teaspoon ground cloves

1 teaspoon ground ginger

1 teaspoon ground aniseed

10 Queen of Reinette apples (peeled, cored & cut into halves)

Crème fraîche

If you feel like baking apples, I really recommend using Queen of Reinette.

In a bowl, put the orange juice, Riesling, sugar and spices. Add the apples and let them marinate for 12 hours. Put the apples in an oven dish and put in the oven at 220°C for 1 hour. Remove from the oven and put in a bowl. Smash the apples gently with a wooden spoon and mix in the juice left in the oven dish.

Serve at room temperature topped with crème fraîche.

COMPOTE: CARAWAY & APPLE COMPÔTE

Difficulty level: easy
Calories: 90
Preparation time: 45 minutes

Serves 4

1kg Canada apple

60g unsalted butter

100g caster sugar

2 teaspoon crushed caraway seeds

100ml dry white wine

300ml water

Always use very ripe fruit – you must also use the most flavoursome apples available, such as Elstar or Canada.

Peel and cut the apples into 8. Remove any hard parts and make sure to remove any seeds. Wash under cold water. Melt the butter in a thick-bottomed pan and add the apple. Stir and add the sugar. Carry on stirring until the sugar looks like it has melted. Add the caraway seeds and the white wine.

Reduce the white wine until it has almost completely evaporated and add the water. Cover and cook at a very slow simmer for 12 minutes.

The apples should have turned mushy. Break them even more with a spoon while making sure that the remaining liquid evaporates. Refrigerate and serve very cold. Delicious when mixed with yogurt.

RAW APPLE

Beef & Jonagold carpaccio

Difficulty level: medium
Calories: 120
Preparation time: 10 minutes

I love raw apple with my meat. I think that beef and raw apple are meant to be served together. Thinly sliced apple on top of raw beef carpaccio is delicious. The best apples for this purpose are the Jonagold or Boskoop. They are tightly fibred, a little acidic and very juicy.

Serves 4

250g beef fillet

8 Jonagold apples

1 lemon (juiced)

½ pink shallot

100ml olive oil

50ml balsamic vinegar

Salt & pepper

Cut the beef fillet into very thin slices and divide between 4 large plates. Peel and core the apples. Slice them very thinly and pour a little lemon juice over them.

Slice the shallot very thinly and divide it between the 4 plates. Add the olive oil, balsamic vinegar, salt and black pepper.

Do not wait too long to serve this dish once it is ready, as the apples will very quickly turn dark and the vinegar will start cooking the beef.

FAT DUCK APPLE

Difficulty level: medium
Calories: 230
Preparation time: 45 minutes

Apple and foie gras have always been a match made in heaven. The richness of the foie gras married with the slight acidity of the apple is a perfect balance. It is almost like a man and a woman. Adam and Eve! Here, for once, the apple is on top.

Serves 4

- 4 Royal Gala apples
- Salt
- 200ml port
- 2 tablespoons honey
- 2 white onions
- 50ml olive oil
- 4 slices duck foie gras (50g each or 1.5cm thick)
- 2 sprigs thyme
- 1 sprig parsley (chopped)

Wash the apples and cut them width-ways in 2. Remove the peduncle, making sure you don't break the apple.

Boil the apples in a little salted water for 3 minutes. Remove and lay the apples on an oiled roasting tray.

Cook in the oven with the door ajar at 160°C for 25 minutes until the apples are soft but not mushy.

In a pan, boil the port together with the honey until reduced to a thick consistency.

Peel and thinly slice the onions. Slowly cook in a pan with the olive oil, while almost constantly stirring, until the onions are soft and slightly brown.

Remove the onions from the pan and in the same pan, fry the slices of foie gras after having salted them on both sides. The heat must be very strong so the fois gras is seared rather than boiled. Cook the foie gras for 1 minute on each side and remove.

Once the apples are ready, reconstruct the apple by putting the bottom half of the apple at the bottom, topped with the foie gras, onion and the top half of the apple – just like a burger in its bun.

Add a little fresh thyme and chopped parsley, and recreate the stem of the apple with some parsley stalks. Pour the reduction of port and honey over each apple.

GRANNY'S SORBET

Granny Smith & black sesame seeds

Difficulty level: easy
Calories: 120
Preparation time: 3½ hours

Serves 4

20g black sesame seeds

200ml water

200g sugar

5g pectin powder

1 litre Granny Smith apple juice

1 lemon (juiced)

Set the oven to grill and slightly toast the sesame seeds.

Start by bringing the water and sugar to the boil.

Add the sesame seeds.

Add the pectin powder and chill for 3 hours.

Add the apple juice and the lemon juice.

Turn in an ice-cream machine.

If you don't have an ice-cream machine, you can freeze the mixture and scratch it with a fork as it becomes frozen. It will turn into a delicious granité.

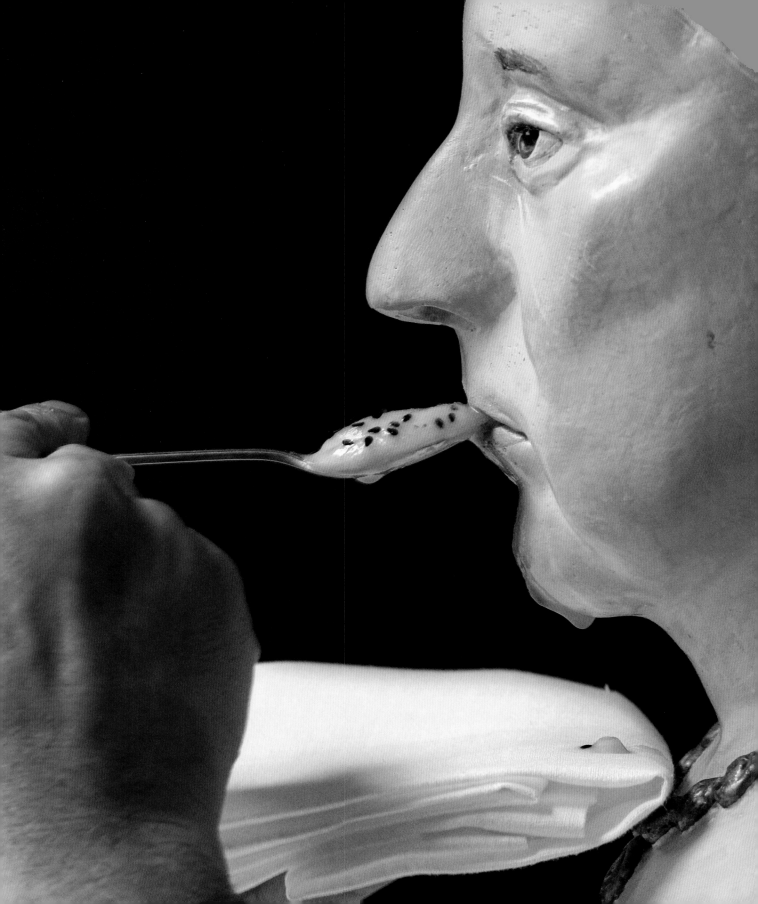

APRICOT

It is funny how an apricot transforms itself during its exposure to the sun.

It can be eaten very early in the season (say mid-June) for those who love acidity, or can be eaten very late (end of August).

The apricot is very familiar to me. The south of France is a large producer of apricots and I can remember them being part of our meal throughout the summer.

It is quite hard to find a perfect apricot, and we should always bite into it before deciding what to do with it. It is not rare to find some beautiful-looking apricots that taste too ripe or too acidic, or whose flesh is too white (even though their skin is deep orange).

What I really love about apricots is that it is never too late or too early in the season to enjoy them.

An acidic apricot is great when poached in syrup or done as a crumble with lots of sugar.

A freshly picked apricot (tight skin, tender flesh and perfect balance of sweet and acidity) is only good when eaten raw and on its own.

And when they are very ripe, it is usually best to make them into jam. Is there a better summery jam than an apricot one? No way.

APRICOT

ACIDIC EARLY-SEASON APRICOT CRUMBLE

Difficulty level: medium
Calories: 450
Preparation time: 1 hour

Serves 4

150g unsalted butter

200g caster sugar

60g ground almonds

16 apricots (keep the apricot stones as they can be really useful in a kitchen. See below)

3 eggs

Pinch of salt

2 tablespoons rum

60g flour

Brown sugar

200ml single cream

In a large hot pan, brown half of the butter. Add half of the sugar, ground almonds and the apricots (cut in half). Toss them for 3 to 4 minutes and put on a very low heat. Cover with a lid. You may have to add half a glass of water if it starts getting too dry.

Meanwhile mix the eggs, the remaining butter, sugar, salt, rum and flour together until you get a crumbly dough.

When the apricots are cooked, remove them from the pot and let them cool.

Lay the apricots in a large dish, making sure to pour the cooking jus over.

Break the crumble over them, covering up to 1.5cm thick. Sprinkle some brown sugar over it. The dough should be 1.5cm high on top of the apricots. Cook in an oven at 180°C for 7 minutes in grill position.

Serve warm with some single cream on the side.

ARICOT GRANITÉ

Difficulty level: easy
Calories: 300
Preparation time: 6 hours

Serves 4

1 litre water

150g sugar

20 apricot stones

250g prawns (cooked & peeled)

40g broken peanuts

20ml olive oil

Black pepper

Boil the water and the sugar together. Add the apricot stones and let them infuse until cold, then place in the freezer. Scratch the surface of the frozen apricot syrup with a fork every hour.

In a frozen Martini glass, put a third of granité. Top with some prawns and sprinkle some broken peanuts. Add a dash of olive oil and some cracked black pepper.

Serve as a starter.

APRICOT, CHICKPEAS & CORIANDER

Difficulty level: medium
Calories: 140
Preparation time: 30 minutes

Serves 4

20g butter

12 apricots

120g cooked chickpeas

40g shallots (chopped)

50ml olive oil

2 tablespoons white wine vinegar

Salt & pepper

½ bunch fresh coriander (chopped)

40g bran flakes

Slowly warm your butter in a pan until it turns brown. Add the apricots, cut in half, and gently cook them until the skin starts detaching itself and the apricot turns mushy. Slowly stir for 5 minutes and remove from the heat. Let the apricots cool.

In a large vegetable bowl, mix together the chickpeas, shallots, olive oil, vinegar, salt and pepper.

Gently add the apricots, making sure not to break them too much. The flesh must keep a little bit of texture.

Serve in a soup plate and add the chopped coriander and sprinkle over some bran flakes.

I hope that you kept every single apricot stone you were ready to throw away.

When the apricot season ends, I sometimes find myself craving its flavour. That is when I infuse the apricot stones in syrup and make a granité out of it. It is dead simple, yet it has a wonderful depth of flavour.

AVOCADO

When I left France in 1995, and after spending many years in gastronomic restaurants covered in Michelin stars, I had absolutely no idea that you could actually 'do' something with avocado.

Avocados were invisible in the restaurants where I had worked. If you wanted to be taken seriously, you could not have avocado on your menu. That was the norm.

One of the worst insults I was subjected to, when at Ducasse, was to be told that I was only good to cook avocado. Obviously, that would make the entire brigade laugh and would make me look very small, and the head chef very big. Not a nice man, but I've touched on that before.

Don't get me wrong, I had eaten avocado at home in the '80s, my mother sometimes served it. She would simply prepare it with a classic vinaigrette as a starter, but that was it.

Avocado was at this time the perfect example of food you would find on a motorway – served with tiny prawns, shredded lettuce and covered in cocktail sauce. Back then no combination with another ingredient had transformed or enhanced this fruit.

So when I started working as a private chef in San Francisco in September 1995 my boss, who had been brought up on delicious Californian avocado all his life, asked me to prepare some. I wanted to impress him: I wanted to show him that I was a creative and talented young French chef who could transform anything into something exceptional. So I decided to cook the most disgusting thing I have ever done: hot avocado flan. It was worse than anything one could imagine. It was extremely bitter and weird in texture with a horrible grey-blue colour. But being French and proud (and stupid), I decided to serve it. My boss was very forgiving and accepted my apology on the basis that avocado was an exotic product for me. I went through a long and delicious educational process after that which opened many of my closed brain cells!

During the avocado season, which lasts from November to May, I love mixing them with fresh citrus fruit, marinated fatty fish and even crispy duck skin. I still love my avocado vinaigrette, but there are so many other wonderful things you can do with avocado that it is a pity to just stop there.

To be good, an avocado has to be ripe. I have learnt over the years to be patient in order to get the perfect texture. It is a difficult act to balance as sometimes a day or two can make all the difference. When I look for the best avocado, I usually only buy the ones you can touch. I need to weigh them in my hand. If they feel heavy, with very shiny skins, free of any stains, it is usually a good sign. Then I usually check at the base if the peduncle is very fixed or starts moving a bit. Then I slightly press on its skin, making sure not to break it. If there is a slight light resistance it probably means that the avocado is soon going to be perfect. I double-check by slightly shaking the fruit. If I feel that the stone is moving a little bit, it means it is ripe. That is the one I buy.

AVOCADO & QUINOA SALAD

Pink grapefruit, mint & fennel

Difficulty level: medium
Calories: 260
Preparation time: 40 minutes

Serves 4

- 2 pink grapefruits (peeled, segmented & juiced)
- 3 tablespoons Xeres vinegar
- 1 tablespoon Dijon mustard
- 100ml olive oil
- Salt & pepper
- 4 baby fennel (washed & thinly sliced with a Japanese mandolin)
- 120g quinoa (cooked for 8 minutes in boiling salted water, drained & refreshed)
- 20 mint leaves (washed & thinly chopped)
- 4 Hass avocados

Peel and segment the grapefruit, reserving 3 tablespoons of the juice for the dressing. In a large bowl start by preparing the dressing. Pour the grapefruit juice together with the Xeres vinegar. Add the mustard and whisk the mixture.

Add the olive oil, salt, pepper, the sliced fennel, quinoa and mint leaves.

Stir and taste. Add salt if needed.

Open the avocados, remove their stones and spoon them out from their skins. Slice them and divide them between 4 large plates. Place the quinoa mix and the grapefruit segments over them.

Add more chopped mint and serve.

AVOCADO, WATERCRESS & CELERY

Difficulty level: easy
Calories: 280
Preparation time: 40 minutes

Serves 4

- 200ml balsamic vinegar
- 100ml water
- 1 tablespoon caster sugar
- 1 celery head (cleaned & washed)
- 1 bunch watercress
- 4 Hass avocados
- 1 lemon (zest & juice)
- 50g tub of fat-free cream
- Salt & pepper

Start this recipe by reducing the balsamic vinegar which is going to be used at the end of this dish. In a thick-bottomed pan, reduce the balsamic vinegar with the water and the caster sugar by half.

The balsamic is going to get a little bit thicker and a lot more powerful. Leave it to cool.

Thinly slice the head of celery with a mandolin and keep the pieces in icy water for 30 minutes so they turn very crunchy. It is important that the celery gets this texture in order to balance the softness of the avocado in the finished dish.

Remove the leaves from the watercress and clean them. Dry them out and keep them in the fridge until just before serving.

Open the avocados and remove their stones. Put them on a chopping board and cut them into thin slices with a very sharp knife.

Divide them onto 4 large plates. Put the crunchy celery (which you will have dried and quickly seasoned with the lemon juice) over them and cover with the fat-free cream. Add the watercress leaves, grated lemon skins and spoon some dollops of the balsamic vinegar reduction.

Add some salt and pepper and serve immediately.

CHERRY

There was a tradition in my family around the middle of June: as soon as the cherries were ripe, we were sent to our friends who had some magnificent cherry trees and were told to climb on the trees and eat as much as we wanted. We were left alone for an entire afternoon and we used to eat so much that for the next 4 days we would have tummy ache and we wouldn't dare eat any more for the rest of the season!

This way our parents were sure that we were not going to eat too many cherries through the season. It is well known that cherries are extremely high in sugar and therefore very bad for us!

What they probably didn't know is that the cherry usually relieves headache and is also a natural antiseptic.

How can I be sure to find the best cherry? Despite the fact that I have been over-eating cherries for many years, I am still very excited to see them come back in June.

I get very upset when I see them around Christmas when they are brought from Chile – even more annoying is the fact they are sometimes extremely good!

The first cherry I eat should be the template of what I expect for the rest of the season.

I enjoy waiting and choosing the one that is going to be the first to pop into my mouth. I have to enjoy my first cherry – but I want to have the best. I will wait until the moment I come across the one that is going to tell me: eat me! I am the perfect one for you.

A dark colour, a tight but slightly soft skin, shiny with some blurry reflections.

I take it into my fingers I inspect it, I am very careful, I prepare my mouth to receive it, I send a message to my brain telling it to be prepared to taste the first cherry of the year. I put it in my mouth and press on its skin with my teeth. The skin should break firmly and release its juice through my teeth. I would then swallow the juice and palpate the texture left with my tongue. Suddenly I would feel the stone and make it roll on my tongue in order to remove the flesh that sticks on it.

I would swallow the flesh and breathe through my nose.

Then I would spit out the stone – don't swallow it!

The retro-olfaction of the cherry will fix the taste onto my brain and will remind me what the taste of a perfect cherry should be: dark, red and juicy.

CHERRY

ROASTED CHERRIES WITH RIESLING *(Pictured)*

Difficultty level: easy
Calories: 205
Preparation time: 1 hour

Serves 4

- 200ml dry Riesling
- 1 teaspoon ground cinnamon
- 1 teaspoon ground ginger
- 80g brown sugar
- 1 orange (zest)
- 200g cherries
- 4 tablespoons crème fraîche

Preheat the oven to 170°C.

Whisk the Riesling with the spices. Then add the sugar and continue whisking until the sugar has completely dissolved. Add the zest of the orange.

Into a buttered baking tray, tip the cherries and cover them with the Riesling and spice mix. Cover with aluminium foil and cook for 30 minutes. Make sure you shake the tray from time to time.

Serve either hot or cold with a large spoonful of crème fraîche over the cherries.

GRANDMA'S CHERRY CLAFOUTIS

Difficulty level: medium
Calories: 370
Preparation time: 1 hour

Serves 4

- 400g flour
- 250g sugar
- Pinch salt
- 2 drops white wine vinegar
- 8 eggs
- 1 litre milk
- 100 whipping cream
- 2 handfuls almost-over cherries
- 10ml kirsch

Preheat the oven to 180°C. Put the flour, sugar, salt and vinegar in a big bowl. Whisk them together and add the eggs one at a time. Pour in the milk and the whipping cream while whisking.

Butter a large pie dish. Rinse the cherries and spread them all over the dish. Pour the mix over and put in the oven for 35 minutes.

Serve warm with a bit of kirsch and a spoonful of whipped cream on each plate.

Remember that the cherries should be cooked with their stones in.

I get very upset when I see cherries around Christmas when they are brought from Chile – even more annoying is the fact they are sometimes extremely good!

JOLLY JELLY BABY

Raspberry & mint flavoured jelly baby

Difficulty level: medium
Calories: 270
Preparation time:1 hours 30 minutes Freezing: 24 hours

Taste, texture, and most importantly shape, are constantly on my mind when I try to inspire kids and get them interested in creating dishes. I have recently found some amazing pastry moulds made out of silicone. They are great for bringing a bit of creativity and sometimes eccentricity to what could otherwise be a boring dish. At the end of the book there is a list of suppliers where you can find ways to be creative with your cooking.

Serves 4

Raspberry jus

100ml water

80g caster sugar

400g fresh raspberries

Jelly

9 gelatine leaves

500ml water

100ml mint syrup

150g sugar

2 teaspoons peppermint essence

For the raspberry jus

Boil the water together with the sugar. As soon as it boils, remove from the heat and let it cool. In a blender, blend the raspberries until liquified and add the cool syrup.

Place in the freezer and let it freeze for at least 5 hours. After 5 hours, try to stretch it into a long shape and put it back in the freezer for a minimum of 12 hours.

Making the jelly

Boil the sugar, water and mint syrup together. Remove from the stove as soon as it boils and let it cool for 5 minutes.

Add the gelatine leaves and the peppermint essence and gently stir, making sure that the gelatine is well dissolved. Wait until the syrup is at room temperature and start filling the jelly baby mould. Only fill ¾ of its volume and let it almost set in the fridge for 2 hours.

Take it out of the fridge and place the frozen raspberry purée inside. Cover with the remaining unset mint jelly and keep in the fridge to finish setting for at least 8 hours.

Removing the jelly from the mould should not be too hard. However, if you experience difficulties, just sit the mould in hot water for 30 seconds.

MARINATED FIGS IN SANGRIA

Difficulty level: medium
Calories: 285
Preparation time: 1 hour

The fig has always been a main part of my nutrition. We had a huge fig tree at our house in Avignon and I remember my mother endlessly preparing fig jam when the fruit was over-ripe. We just couldn't eat all the fruit. Figs can get so sweet that you almost don't have to add sugar to the jam. The figs get the sun during the whole summer – it is only in September that you can really appreciate them when they are dark and very soft.

Serves 4

Sangria

500ml red wine

75g sugar

1 orange (halved)

1 lemon (halved)

½ cinnamon stick

½ vanilla pod

3 figs

40g sugar

40g butter

8 large figs

It is not an easy fruit to enjoy. Its consistency is quite weird. My sister used to be scared by its flesh. During my time with Alain Ducasse, I realised that the fig can be a top-quality ingredient and can be present on a 3-Michelin-star menu. I really respect this fruit; it is the symbol of what summer has left behind – a lot of sun transformed into sugar through the fruit.

In a large pot combine the red wine, sugar, orange, lemon, cinnamon and vanilla. Bring to the boil.

When it is boiling, add the figs, remove from the heat and let them marinate until the sangria cools.

Into a little saucepan, put the sugar and butter. Slowly heat it and wait until it reaches caramelisation. Add the figs and roll them in the caramel very slowly for less than a minute.

Cut the figs in half, put them in a soup plate and cover with the sangria.

You can eat this warm or cold.

COMPÔTE OF FIGS & ALMOND

Difficulty level: medium
Calories: 150
Preparation time: 2 hours 20 minutes

Serves 4

As many late-season figs as you can find

Ground almonds (a third of the volume of the figs)

Caster sugar (a third of the volume of the figs, and extra for frying the bread)

Water (a third of the volume of the figs)

Some thick slices of Pain de Campagne

20g butter

I usually do this compôte without washing the figs, but I would recommend washing them before using.

Put the figs into a large pan on a low heat and smash them with a wooden spoon. Add the ground almonds and carry on stirring. Pour in the sugar and the water. Cover and let them cook at a very slow simmer.

Make sure that the mixture cooks very slowly and that it doesn't burn at the bottom of the pan. After 2 hours of cooking, remove the cover and evaporate the water that may be left on top.

Cut the bread into thick finger shapes. In a pan, add a teaspoon of butter and sugar. When the butter starts turning brown, add the bread to the pan and cook on both sides until it turns golden brown.

Cover the bread with the fig jam. You can also add some honey, yogurt or crème fraîche.

The compôte can be frozen for future use or kept in the fridge for no more than 5 days.

GRAPE

The grape is one of the oldest known cultivated fruits. It is grown for wine making and for the table. Its colour starts from palest green up to dark ruby red. I have always been a grape fan. Its taste has always appealed to me as far back as I can remember. I am actually quite sad not to remember the day I fell in love with grapes. How old was I? Who made me eat my first grape? No idea. My memory cannot go as far back as I would like sometimes. So I spend most years refusing to eat grapes until I can get hold of the first grape the of the season in mid-August. It is such a reward for me. I am always so proud not to have bastardised my love for grapes with something from the other side of the world: a seedless little bowl of sugar which does not remotely taste of real grape. When I see my kids raving about their grapes in February, I just want to cry. Seriously!

FRESH GRAPES (IN SEASON)

Difficulty level: easy

Serves 1

Grapes

Remember that the best way to appreciate grapes is to eat them on their own. With nothing else!

Make sure you know the kind of grape that you love and just indulge.

SAUTÉED GRAPES & ELDERFLOWER

Difficulty level: medium
Calories: 110
Preparation time: 50 minutes

Serves 4

10g butter

400g slightly off & starting to get soft grapes (washed & removed from their stalks)

100ml white wine (Sauvignon)

1 tablespoon elderflower cordial

1 handful elderflower flowers

When the grapes are going slightly off, it is time to do something with them. This recipe brings together two ingredients that complement each other very well. The over-sweetness of an old grape will be balanced by the subtlety and deepness of flavour of the elderflower. It is like chewing a glass of Sauvignon!

Melt the butter in a hot pan and start tossing the grapes in it. Make sure the heat is very low and gentle. Add the white wine and the cordial. Boil and reduce half of the liquid.

Remove from the heat and divide into 4 low tumblers and cover with the fresh elderflowers. Serve immediately.

LEMON LAYER PUDDING

Difficulty level: medium
Calories: 380
Preparation time: 1 hour

Only after spending many years wondering about the qualities of the lemon, I realised it was a very subtle fruit. A fruit that needs to be understood before being judged! A fruit that is very strong on its own and the perfect partner for many things. Chewing a lemon is a great experience: it is very acidic at the beginning but then when your tastebuds get used to it, you will realise that the taste is so concentrated that it is going to stay in your mouth for ages after swallowing.

Serves 4

- 80g unsalted butter
- 2 lemons (zest & juice)
- 160g sugar
- 2 eggs (separated)
- 200ml full-fat milk
- 60g self-raising flour
- Pinch of salt
- 10ml sour Activia jogurt

My favourite is the lemon from Menton in the south of France where they make a lemon so sweet that you can almost eat it like an apple!

Preheat the oven to 170°C.

In a bowl, whisk the butter, lemon juice, lemon zest and sugar. Cream the mixture until it looks pale and a little fluffy. Add the egg yolks and beat well. Stir in the milk.

Fold in the flour and the salt. Whisk the egg white until stiff and fold in carefully with the other ingredients.

Pour into a buttered ovenproof dish (or the Pac-Man silicone mould, pictured). Stand the dish in a shallow tin of water and cook at the top of the oven for 40 minutes. The top of the lemon cake should be firm to touch. Serve warm with a spoonful of yogurt.

PEPPERED LEMON INFUSION

Sugared celery & cucumber

Difficulty level: easy
Calories: 140
Preparation time: 1 hour

Serves 4

3 bunches celery hearts

1 litre water

180g caster sugar

1 bunch lemongrass

2 gelatine leaves

4 lemons (zest & juice)

½ bunch mint

20g Sarawak pepper

Slice the celery into long, thin juliennes. Keep them in ice-cold water for 10 minutes until they become crunchy.

Boil the water with the sugar and the lemongrass. Boil for 5 minutes and let it cool down for 5 minutes.

Add the gelatine leaves, the lemon zest and let it cool down until it is at room temperature. Add the lemon juice.

Pass through a sieve and divide the infusion between 4 large bowls.

Chop the fresh mint and mix it with the julienne of celery .

Place the celery in the middle of each bowl and refrigerate until the liquid looks a little set.

Grind pepper over just before serving.

MELON

In her book *An Omelette and a Glass of Wine*, Elizabeth David tells of her experience in the Cavaillon fruit and vegetable market. She describes the early morning and the very strong smell of melon.

When I read it, I could easily smell it too: the melon gives off a very particular fragrance. During the melon season (May/June – early July) Cavaillon becomes its world capital. (At least that is what I thought until I discovered that there were other places in the world that grew melon!)

The Charentais or Cavaillon melon is the best type of melon and in order to recognise if it is good or not, you need to smell it 'au cul' (from the ass).

When I was first told this, I didn't really understand why I should smell it from somewhere other than from my nose. I should have understood that it meant the melon 'cul' Not mine!

If it smells strong, very settled and pure then it is good. If it smells light, a green smell and slightly sharp then you should wait. If it smells like alcohol then it is too late. Easy, no?

If your melon is perfect then you have made the right choice. So eat it as it is. You do not need to add anything: no Port, no Italian ham – nothing.

If your melon is too green, you should wait. Be patient as melons always ripen with age (unlike fruit from trees, like peaches).

If your melon is too ripe, you can make a purée and serve it as a pudding or even freeze it and make a granité.

MELON SOUP & FRESH GOATS' CHEESE

Difficulty level: easy
Calories: 150
Preparation time: 1 hour Resting: 3 hours

Serves 4

- **100g fresh goats' cheese**
- **30g fresh ricotta cheese**
- **100ml olive oil**
- **Black pepper**
- **1 lime (juiced)**
- **Salt**
- **1 over-ripe melon**

In a bowl, mix the fresh goats' cheese and ricotta cheese with the olive oil and the black pepper. You need to turn them into a thick paste. Add the juice of 1 lime and add a little bit of salt. Taste and refrigerate.

Cut the melon in 2 and remove all the seeds and small filaments attached to it. Spoon out the flesh into the bowl of a blender. Blend quickly until all the lumps have disappeared. Do not blend too much as this will make the soup turn brown. Transfer the soup into a bowl and refrigerate for at least 3 hours before serving.

Make some small quenelles with the goats' cheese mix and divide them between 4 soup plates. Serve the melon soup around them. Add the black pepper at the end and serve.

MELON GRANITÉ, MINT PURÉE & SOFT TOFU

Difficulty level: medium
Calories: 80
Preparation time: 1 hour 30 minutes Resting: 2 hours

Serves 4

1 large over-ripe melon

½ bunch fresh mint

1 lemon (zest)

80g soft Japanese tofu

Cut the melon in 2 and remove all the seeds and filaments attached to it. Spoon out the flesh into the bowl of a blender. Blend quickly until all the lumps have disappeared. Do not blend too much as this will make the mixture turn brown.

Transfer it to a deep flat tray and freeze. Scratch the surface of the frozen melon purée every 2 to 3 hours until it turns into a granité.

Clean the blender and mix the mint leaves and the lemon zest. Slice the tofu to ½-cm pieces. Divide the slices among 4 soup plates.

Cover with the granité and pour the mint purée over it.

ORANGE MARMALADE

Difficulty level: easy
Calories: 45 per spoon
Preparation time: 1 hour

My great grandmother used to tell me that she would get only two oranges for Christmas as her present. And then she found it thrilling to be able to eat the oranges! The orange is now very commonly used and consumed. It is rich in vitamin C and is indispensable for our immune systems. When the orange is brightly coloured, it means that it is very rich in carotene, which is very good for anti-cancer and anti-ageing. The more acidic the orange, the better it is for a good balance of our metabolism.

Makes 20 spoonfuls

- 100g butter
- 350g sugar
- 20 oranges (washed & roughly chopped into smallish cubes)
- 250ml water

The orange is rich in pectin and can help reduce your cholesterol. A good orange is only 74 calories: that is about the same as one low-fat yogurt.

The problem with oranges these days is that they are far too sprayed with pesticide and you really need to wash them before eating. I have recently started to use a natural product called Veggi Wash which claims to remove pesticides from fruits and vegetables. I am still alive so . . .

In a large pot, put the butter and sugar on a high heat.

When the sugar starts turning brown, add the chopped oranges, reduce the heat and stir for 5 minutes. Add the water, cover and cook until ready (this usually takes 45 minutes).

You may have to add a bit of water from time to time.

The best way to eat orange marmalade is with freshly toasted sourdough bread and clotted cream.

ORANGE, TOFU & YUZU CURD

Difficulty level: hard
Calories: 140
Preparation time: 1 hour

Serves 4

- 4 large oranges
- Pinch salt
- 1 lime (juiced)
- 30g unsalted butter
- 30g flour
- 2 gelatine leaves
- 250g soft tofu
- 4 large green shiso leaves (cleaned & thinly chopped)
- 200ml yuzu
- Pepper

Cut the tops off the oranges and remove their flesh delicately, making sure not to break the skin.

Clean the orange peel 'shells' and keep in the freezer to stabilise their colour.

Pour the flesh into a blender and mix it very quickly with the salt and the lime juice. Do not over blend the orange as we want to keep a little bit of substance to it.

In a warm pan on the stove, melt the butter with the flour until it starts drying it out and looking bubbly. Pour in the orange pulp and stir for 3 minutes. Bring it to the boil and transfer the contents of the pan to another bowl, add the gelatine leaves, stir and leave to cool.

When cooled, add the tofu and mix with a fork. Add the chopped shiso leaves and the yuzu.

Take the oranges out of the freezer and fill them with the mixture.

Add some freshly cracked black pepper and serve.

Yuzu is a citrus fruit mainly used in Japanese cooking and tastes like a combination of grapefruit, sweet orange and lemon put together.

Green shiso is a bit citrussy, with a hint of basil.

ORANGE BLOSSOM MARSHMALLOW

Difficulty level: hard
Calories: 90
Preparation time: 1 hour Setting time: 2 hours

Serves 4

500ml water

50g gelatine leaves

1 tablespoon lemon juice

225ml orange blossom water

400g glucose

600g icing sugar

Cornflour mixed with icing sugar for dusting

Divide the water in 2. Boil in 2 pans. Remove one from the heat and dissolve the gelatine and transfer to a mixing bowl. Add the lemon juice and the orange blossom water.

Add the glucose and sugar to the other pot of boiling water and bring the mixture to 116°C.

When the temperature is reached, slowly pour the hot sugar solution in a thin stream into the gelatine solution, beating all the time. Continue to beat until the maximum volume is reached (for about 5 minutes).

Pour the mixture into a tray dusted with icing sugar and cornflour. Leave to set for 2 hours.

When set, cut into cubes and dust the pieces in a mixture of icing sugar and cornflour.

PEACH

If there was one fruit I could describe as the King of Summer Fruit, it would be the peach. The peach is seasonally right. I mean that when the peach is ready to be eaten is when you need it the most.

During my childhood, I knew that after the strawberries, the peaches would come and this would mean eating outside almost every night in the garden with my parents. Hot days and warm evenings in the south of France.

What I needed then to re-hydrate my body was something juicy and slightly sweet, easy to eat and affordable. The peach was the answer. And I was dead lucky to be able to help myself directly from the trees – which did not actually belong to me or my parents.

So I got caught helping myself!

A farmer, who didn't really like the idea of me eating his peaches, caught me red-handed (well, light pink-handed actually). He should have been so grateful that I was only eating the perfectly ripened ones, the juiciest ones – it was a sign of me recognising the great job he had done on his peaches. He didn't! He chased me and caught me and made sure that I would never do it again. I was so frightened. I never did it again.

The peach is originally from China but was brought to Europe by the Persians. Louis XIV was a peach lover and gave the name to his favourite 'Téton de Venus' or 'Venus nipples' (I like those very kitsch names; French kings sometimes had a lot of finesse).

My favourite has always been the vine peach or *pêche de vigne*. This type is the tastiest and my grandmother wouldn't eat any other peach but this one.

I was very lucky to be able to eat those little peaches because it is very rare to find them. The white peach (its near cousin) is almost as good and is easier to find in July and August at a high-street supermarket.

I have seen people not touching, feeling or smelling their peaches before buying them. I wonder how they eat them. Do they eat them like an apple? I mean crunchy? I hope not! Supermarkets should employ peach choosers in season to guide people how to make their choices. I am sure that we would consume more peaches.

The peach is also lucky to be one of the healthiest fruits around. Very low in calories, rich in fibre, potassium and is good to balance your metabolism.

3 SIMPLE WAYS TO EAT PEACHES

Difficulty level: easy
Calories: 150
Preparation time: 3 hours 30 minutes

UNDER-RIPE PEACHES

Serves 4

4 unripe peaches

100ml olive oil

2g salt

30g sugar

2g pepper

8 raw prawns

5g unsalted butter

3 tablespoons Xeres vinegar

50ml prawn jus

Semi-dried peaches, prawn & Xeres vinegar

Cut the peaches into quarters and put them on a plate with olive oil, salt, sugar and pepper. Put them in a very low temperature oven (90°C) for 3 hours until they are semi-dry while retaining a bit of moisture.

In a hot pan, add a spoonful of olive oil. When the oil starts smoking, add the prawns and cook them for 1 minute on each side. Lower the heat and add the butter. Toss the prawns and remove them. Put the pan back on the heat and add the Xeres vinegar and the prawn jus. Reduce a little and pour over the prawns.

You can add them to a green leaf salad or pair with a grilled fish. The peach taste will concentrate during the cooking process and will bring another dimension to the fish.

PEFECTLY RIPE PEACHES

Nothing much to do! Quickly wash it under room-temperature water.

Bite into the peach and let the juice slightly drip off your mouth – as if you were drinking some . . . well, I can't think of anything to add! I like the feeling of the warm, tender, cat-tongue-like peach skin that explodes under the pressure of my teeth and releases the cold juice in my mouth.

So sexy!

OVER-RIPE PEACHES

Calories: 95
Preparation time: 5 minutes

Serves 1

Prosecco

1 peach

Don't worry, it is the best reason to prepare the famous Bellini cocktail. First, explode the peach in your hand over a large glass. Rinse your hand with Prosecco over the glass.

Stir a bit and drink very cold.

PEAR

My earliest memory of a pear was the sight of one sitting in a thin clear bottle in the cabinet we used to have in my parents' dining room. Funnily enough, I never thought then that it could have been the same fruit as the one I loved in purée when I was very young.

My parents adored pear alcohol. There wasn't a family dinner not finished by a few small glasses of pear – 'La Poire', it was called. They were all so high by the end of a meal that La Poire sounded like a medicinal drink.

It was good for everything: not putting on weight, better digestion, relaxation, headaches and tummy aches . . . And I am sure that to them it was also good for reducing the hole in the ozone layer, peace on earth and France winning the next football World Cup . . . La Poire was a must!

I am not a big fan of La Poire. I much prefer the original fruit, especially the English Comice pear. It comes slightly later in the pear season, around the beginning of autumn.

Like Bosc pears, Comice are meaty-fleshed and still firm when fully ripe. The French would tell you that Bosc are better because the Comice stay on the tree too long because of the awful English weather. They never seem to ripen. And I would say that it is exactly the reason why they are so superior!

As with strawberries, English pears are a lot tastier and less sugary than the ones from France.

The Comice is ideal for poaching because it resists turning to mush when cooked. On top of that it has the advantage of keeping its skin smooth, and does not crack.

POACHED AND CARAMELISED COMICE PEARS

Difficulty level: medium
Calories: 180
Preparation time: 45 minutes

Serves 4

- 40g caster sugar
- 200ml water
- 1 lemon (juiced)
- 200ml red cooking wine
- 8 Comice pears (peeled & left whole)
- 1 spoonful dark molasses
- 2 tablespoons balsamic vinegar

Put the sugar in large saucepan together with the water.

Put on a low heat and cook until the sugar turns to caramel. Add the lemon juice, and the red wine. Remove from the heat and place the pears in the pan. Add the molasses and the balsamic vinegar and cover.

Cook for 20 minutes at a low heat.

Serve the pears at room temperature covered in their own cooking syrup.

POACHED WILLIAMS PEAR & CHOCOLATE TART

Difficulty level: hard
Calories: 350 (for 2 helpings)
Preparation time: 5 hours

Serves 4

Tart base

- 250g flour
- 10g caster sugar
- 7g table salt
- 180g unsalted butter (cut into big squares at room temperature, softened)
- 1 egg
- 1 tablespoon water

Pears

- 8 Williams pears (peeled & cored)
- 180g caster sugar
- 1.5 litres water
- ½ vanilla pod (cut in 2)

Chocolate filling

- 4 eggs
- 250g ground almonds
- 200ml whipping cream
- 100ml semi-skimmed milk
- Pinch salt
- 100g dark cocoa powder

Making the tart base

In a bowl, mix the flour, sugar, salt and the butter with your hands until you get a crumbly texture. Break in the egg and add the spoonful of water. Continue working the mix until it comes together as a fragile dough.

Remove the dough from the bowl and continue working it in your hands on a clean, floured surface. Do not overwork the dough as it is always better when it is a little crumbled rather than tense and elastic.

Cover with clingfilm and keep in the fridge for at least 4 hours before using.

Poaching the pears

Place the pears in a deep heavy-bottomed pan. Add sugar, water and the vanilla pod. Slowly boil for 15 minutes. Let the pears cool in the cooking syrup.

When cooled, cut them into four and dry them on a clean kitchen cloth.

Making the chocolate filling

In a bowl, whisk the eggs together with the ground almonds. Add the whipping cream and the milk. Add the salt and cocoa powder.

Finishing the tart

Preheat the oven to 180°C. Roll out the dough and place in a buttered 32cm-diameter tart tin. Place the pears on the pastry and cover them with the cocoa and almond mix.

Cook in the oven for 25 minutes.

Serve warm.

PLUM

The English plum is my favourite plum. I can really play with its tastes and textures from late summer until winter. They are robust and have some very subtle flavours. Unlike their Continental counterparts, they tend to hang onto trees much longer. This gives them plenty of time to accentuate their original flavour without being too compromised by the transformation of sun into sugar.

A COOKED VICTORIA

Difficulty level: medium
Calories: 120
Preparation time: 30 minutes

Serves 4

1 Victoria plum per person

2 teaspoons of honey per plum

½ teaspoon cumin seeds

1 teaspoon Cognac per plum

Wash and dry the plums, put them on a baking tray and pour the honey over them.

Add the cumin seeds and the Cognac and put in the oven at 170°C for 20 minutes.

They can be served on their own or with a dollop of Greek yogurt.

A RIPE TRAGEDY

Difficulty level: easy
Calories: 120

Serves 1

1 tragedy plum

If there is one type of plum that should be eaten when ripe and therefore soft, it is the Tragedy. Early Tragedy season plums do not have a strong plum taste. They can actually sometimes be a bit watery.

The end of season ones have taken the sun a lot more and have had time to diffuse their taste from the stone to the flesh. The taste is deep and complicated.

Its skin can be a little bit astringent but behind it is a sweet and thick juice. The longer you wait, the better it becomes.

CARAMELISED GREENGAGE & PASTIS

Fresh goats' cheese

Difficulty level: medium
Calories: 280
Preparation time: 45 minutes

The English greengage (or Reine Claude in French) is a complicated end-of-summer/early-autumn fruit. Where I come from, we would soak them in alcohol – drink the alcohol and throw away the fruits. But that is because I am French! Here, once again, caramelising the fruit is best in order to concentrate the taste and remove a bit of the acidity.

Serves 4

- 250g greengages (cut in 2, stones removed)
- 40g butter
- 20g ground almonds
- 60g brown sugar
- 50ml Pastis
- 80g fresh goats' cheese
- 20g flaked almonds

Cut the greengages in 2 and rinse under cold water. Add a bit of butter to a hot pan and when it turns brown, add the greengages, ground almonds and brown sugar and roast for 3 minutes.

Cover and carry on cooking for an extra 2 minutes, making sure that they don't dry out. Add the Pastis and flambé while stirring the pan so the plums get coated with the Pastis flavour.

Cut some slices of goats' cheese and sandwich them between the halves of greengage making them look like green burgers, and sprinkle over some flaked almonds. Finish them in the oven (grill position) for 2 minutes.

SUGARED QUINCE *Carrot & olive oil*

Difficulty level: hard
Calories: 75
Preparation time: 4 hours

British quinces are certainly the best fruit grown on the island and are perhaps the most unknown and unused. Unripe quinces are unpalatable – their flesh is astringent – but when ripe, their yellow skin has a fragrance similar to pineapple. Quince is the best thing to eat between meals. Classy snack! This amazing taste is somehow lost in cooking. I don't know why the tradition wants us to cook the quince. When ripe, it is the perfect fruit.

Serves 8

40g butter

2 quinces (peeled, cored & roughly cut into large cubes)

2 large carrots (peeled & thickly chopped)

120g brown sugar

100ml olive oil

250ml water

80g caster sugar

A quince is very low in calories (30 calories for 100g) compared to the pear (50 calories for 100g), and it is not very high in sugar (7g compared to 12g for pear). I usually suggest that you eat this fruit raw and very ripe. You do not need a recipe for that!

However, when cooked, the quince is a wonderful vehicle for other flavours to shine. In the restaurant, we found that quince can be very good when served with bergamot oil and carrot leaves. It is also great when mixed with spices – it tends to soften their power.

Into a hot saucepan, add the butter and when it starts foaming, add the quince, carrot, brown sugar, olive oil and water. Cover and cook at a very low heat for 2 hours.

Make sure that you don't over stir during the cooking process, otherwise it will remove some of the taste of the fruit (it sounds weird, but it is the surprising conclusion I came to wondering for many years why it sometimes didn't taste the same).

Once cooked, blitz in a mixer and pour into an oiled tray. Cover with clingfilm and put in the fridge for at least 4 hours so it has time to set.

Once set, cut into large cubes and cover them with caster sugar.

You can store in the fridge for up to 6 days.

WINTER SPICED QUINCE

Crispy pancetta & black pepper

Difficulty level: medium
Calories: 200
Preparation time: 3 hours

Serves 4

- 1 teaspoon clear honey
- 120g brown sugar
- 750ml water
- 4 quinces (peeled, cored & quartered)
- 1 vanilla pod (cut in 4)
- 1 teaspoon ground cinnamon
- 1 lemon (zest)
- 4 whole cloves
- 8 thin pancetta slices
- Black pepper

In a heavy saucepan, dissolve the honey, brown sugar and water. Add the quinces, vanilla pods, cinnamon, the zest of the lemon and the cloves. Bring to a slow simmer and cook for at least 2 hours with a cover.

Pan-fry the slices of pancetta until crispy and rest them on a cloth to remove the excess fat.

On a large plate, place the quinces and the crispy pancetta slices.

Add some cracked pepper just before serving.

WHAT TO DO WHEN THE QUINCE NEVER SEEMS TO RIPEN?

The quince for those who like to wait . . .

You need to buy a very hard quince early in the season. Surround it with some red apples and wait! Wait until the quince becomes softer. Turn it by a quarter every day and wait. You may have to wait for weeks. But when the quince is perfectly ripe, the experience is well worth the wait!

RHUBARB

We, the French, don't understand anything about rhubarb, nor do we know anything about it. I had never seen or heard of rhubarb until the age of 20. So the day I was faced with my first rhubarb, my reaction was: what the hell is this watery, half-finished red celery?

It looked weird and uninspiring for a closed-minded young French chef like me. Seriously, if I was meant to cook this plant, surely Escoffier would have listed it in his *Guide Culinaire*. I looked up my chef's bible and there was nothing starting with the letters 'Rhu' in the index.

Then, when I asked if it was a vegetable or a fruit, nobody really knew about that either. Sorry, but we French don't cook hermaphrodite plants – you are either a vegetable or a fruit.

That was almost 20 years ago and it is time that I apologised for my original treatment of rhubarb. Sorry for having been brought up as a closed-minded, ego-inflated, better than anybody, young French chef twat.

Sorry. Sorry. Sorry.

I have learnt to understand the complexity of rhubarb and have created a seriously stunning combination of rhubarb, lemon and pepper that I sometimes serve with fresh goats' cheese.

COMPÔTE OF RHUBARB

Indonesian pepper & fresh goats' cheese

Difficulty level: easy
Calories: 220
Preparation time: 1 hour Resting: 12 hours

Serves 4

- 1 lemon skin
- 2 teaspoons Indonesian pepper
- 25g butter
- 300g rhubarb (peeled & cut in 2cm thick pieces)
- 60g caster sugar
- 100ml water
- 80g fresh goats' cheese
- Black pepper

Cut a 10cm x 10cm piece of muslin. Put the lemon skin and the Indonesian pepper in the middle. Close it and tie firmly.

In a hot thick-bottomed pan, melt the butter until it turns foamy. Pour the rhubarb in and stir gently, making sure that no colouration is being applied to the rhubarb.

Add the sugar and continue stirring for at least 2 minutes, making sure that the sugar has dissolved. Add the lemon and pepper bag and the water.

Bring it to the boil and slowly cook at a very low heat. The rhubarb will start losing its water so you should never cover this compôte with a lid. After 7 minutes, the rhubarb will have started to look less watery and more like a compôte texture. Remove from the heat and let it cool down.

Transfer into a bowl, cover tightly with clingfilm and keep it in the fridge for at least 12 hours.

Divide the goats' cheese into 4 small bowls. Remove the lemon and spice bag from the rhubarb compôte and serve the compôte on top of the fresh cheese. You can add a spoonful of caster sugar on top of each plate and a little freshly cracked black pepper.

STRAWBERRY

The strawberry grew wild up until 1713 when François Frazier brought a large strawberry crop from Chile. It is the one that we all know and appreciate.

The strawberry is the number one fruit for those who want to lose weight and, together with the kiwi, the richest in vitamin C. The only problem is that it is getting more and more difficult to find good strawberries.

Strawberries are victims of their own success. Everyone loves them and producers and supermarkets now manage to sell them now all year long. I can't really think of any other fruit which is so delicious during its natural season and so disgusting outside it.

A freshly picked strawberry, not over-refrigerated, with a thin skin that looks like it is going to explode always gives off a very delicate aroma. It is subtle, refined and the aroma lingers in your mouth for minutes after you swallow.

They are so unlike out-of-season strawberries, which taste watery, over-refrigerated, and have no particular flavour or depth. They also have a much tougher skin and are quite often not as sugary as the ones you would buy during their natural season.

The strawberry has become a symbol of the 'you want it, you have it' society we live in. It is sad but I am certain that the more refined about our taste we become, the more we should just refuse to buy out-of-season produce and wait for the best local strawberries to be in season.

Patience and evolution are key.

STRAWBERRIES

Granité, sautéed & in their own juice

During the season, I usually find strawberries in three stages. Under-ripe, over-ripe and ripe. These are the best way to eat this fruit under many forms and textures.

THE OVER-RIPE ONES

Difficulty level: medium
Calories: 180
Preparation time: 12 hours

Serves 4

600g over-ripe British strawberries

100g caster sugar

100ml water

Blend the strawberries together with the water and sugar. Transfer them to the freezer in flat containers. Leave it to set for 2 hours.

Scratch the surface of the liquid with a fork every hour to get the granité texture.

THE UNDER-RIPE ONES

Difficulty level: easy
Calories: 135
Preparation time: 10 minutes

Serves 4

600g under-ripe British strawberries

20g butter

60g caster sugar

Rinse them and dry them very well. Put a saucepan on the heat. When hot, add a spoonful of butter. When the butter turns brown, throw in 1 spoonful of sugar and the strawberries. Sauté for 1 minute and serve immediately.

THE RIPE ONES

Difficulty level: medium
Calories: 160
Preparation time: 7 hours

Serves 4

600g over-ripe British strawberries

250ml water

100g sugar

Cut them into quarters and put them in a bowl with the water and the sugar.

Gently toss them and put them in the fridge and wait at least 6 hours before eating.

PERSIMMON

Difficulty level: easy
Calories: 47 (for 40g fruit)
Preparation time: As long you like

There are a few things that remind me of autumn, but the sight of a persimmon tree with its fruit clinging is really characteristic of the season. The south of France is very rich in persimmon trees, especially Avignon and its region. I remember the first time I had a ripe persimmon like it was yesterday. My mother said it would be like eating an oyster. It was like a slippery jelly that lingered in my mouth. It was beautiful.

My sister thought that it was as disgusting as an oyster and she was right. I thought it was as beautiful. The texture of the persimmon doesn't enter my mouth as often as I would like and I would not offer a persimmon to someone I don't know otherwise they may think I am a very kinky person!

Some varieties of persimmon can be eaten while still hard, but the sensations are completely different and it becomes very boring.

I like the Hachiya, a big persimmon that requires full ripening. I like the fact that you have to wait in order to eat it. The fact that you have to touch it every day, sometimes for weeks, before it is ready is super exciting for me. The more you wait, the more precious it becomes.

I would like to have customers who would come every day and ask me whether the persimmons were ripe or not. If not they would say, 'OK, I'll come back tomorrow, and the day after and the day after until the fruit is ready!'

You know the persimmon is ready if when you cut it, a soft and translucent pulp is revealed all the way to the centre of the fruit. Plant a spoon in it and eat slowly. Chew as much as you can and try to savour the experience for as long as possible.

FLAMING PERSIMMON WITH CALVADOS

Difficulty level: easy
Calories: 120
Preparation time: 10 minutes

Serves 4

- **200ml whipping cream**
- **1 tablespoon icing sugar**
- **4 persimmon (perfectly soft, ready to explode)**
- **100ml Calvados**

Whisk the whipping cream in a cold bowl until it starts to firm. Add the icing sugar and whisk one last time to set the cream.

Choose the best persimmon available. When perfectly ripe, remove the skin on the top of the fruit and put it on a serving plate.

In a small pan, slowly heat up the Calvados while making sure not to boil it.

When hot, pour over the persimmon and flambé it.

Serve the cream on the side.

CONVERSIONS

VOLUME

5ml		1 teaspoon
10ml		1 dessert spoon
15ml	½fl oz	1 tablespoon
20ml		
25ml		5 teaspoons
30ml	1fl oz	
40ml	1½fl oz	
50ml		⅕ cup
55ml	2fl oz	
60ml		
70ml	2½fl oz	
80ml		
90ml	3½fl oz	
100ml		⅖ cup
115ml	4fl oz	
130ml	4½fl oz	
140ml	5fl oz	¼ pint

155ml	5½fl oz	
170ml	6fl oz	
185ml	6½fl oz	
200ml	7fl oz	
225ml	8fl oz	
285ml	10fl oz	½ pint
400ml	14fl oz	
425ml	15fl oz	¾ pint
565ml	20fl oz	1 pint
710ml	25fl oz	1¼ pints
850ml	30fl oz	1½ pints
1 litre	35fl oz	1¾ pints

TEMPERATURE

30°C	85°F	
40°C	105°F	
50°C	120°F	
60°C	140°F	
70°C	160°F	
80°C	175°F	
90°C	195°F	
100°C	212°F	
110°C	225°F	Gas mark ¼
130°C	250°F	Gas mark ½
140°C	275°F	Gas mark 1
150°C	300°F	Gas mark 2
170°C	325°F	Gas mark 3
180°C	350°F	Gas mark 4
190°C	375°F	Gas mark 5
200°C	400°F	Gas mark 6
220°C	425°F	Gas mark 7
230°C	450	Gas mark 8

LIQUID & DRY MEASURE

2 tablespoons	1oz	25ml	30g
1 cup	¼ quart	250ml	225g
2 cups	1 pint	500ml	450g
4 cups	32oz	1 litre	
4 quarts	1 gallon	3.75 litres	

Ounces to grams	multiply by 28.35
Teaspoons to millilitres	multiply by 5
Tablespoons to millilitres	multiply by 15
Fluid ounces to millilitres	multiply by 30
Cups to litres	multiply by 0.24

WEIGHT

10g	½oz		250g	9oz
20g	¾oz		300g	10oz
25g	1oz		400g	14oz
50g	2oz		450g	1lb
100g	3oz		500g	lb 2oz
150g	5oz			
200g	6oz			

INGREDIEN

TS

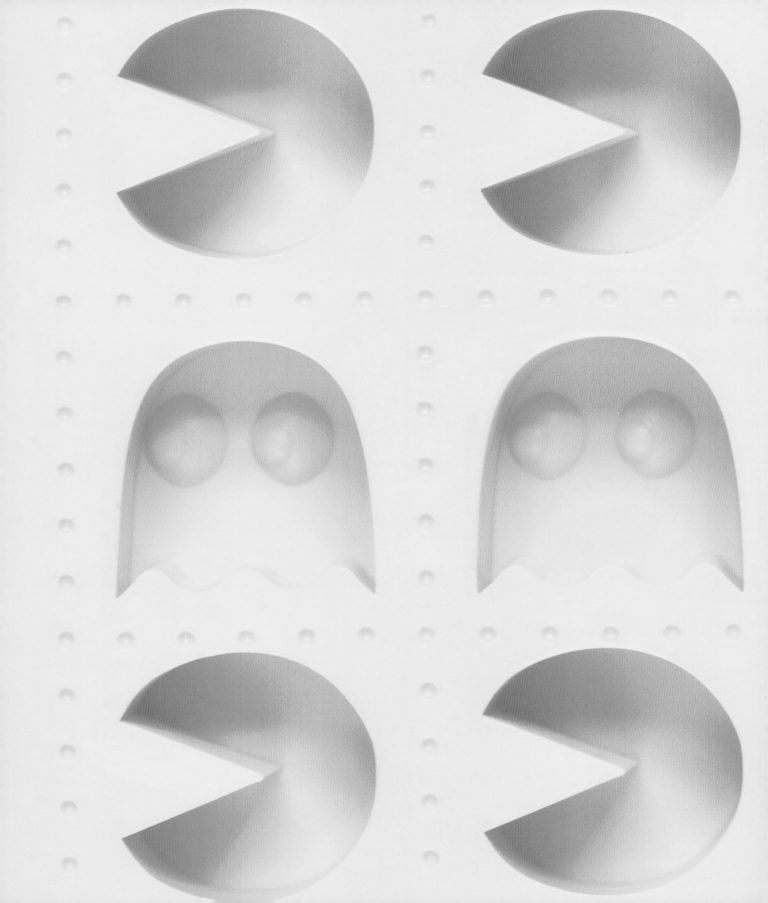

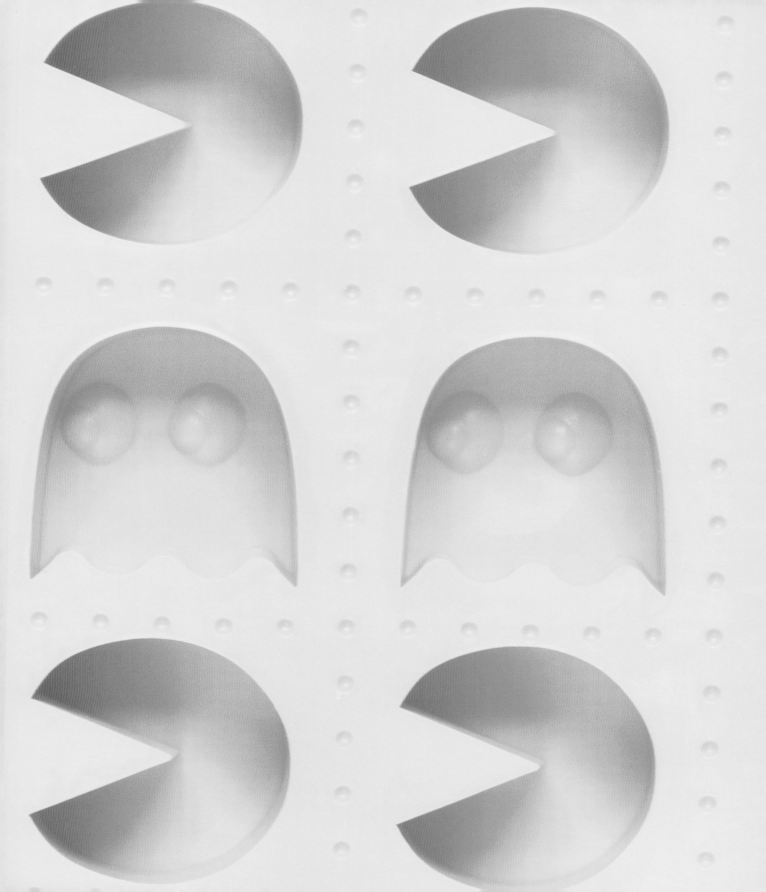

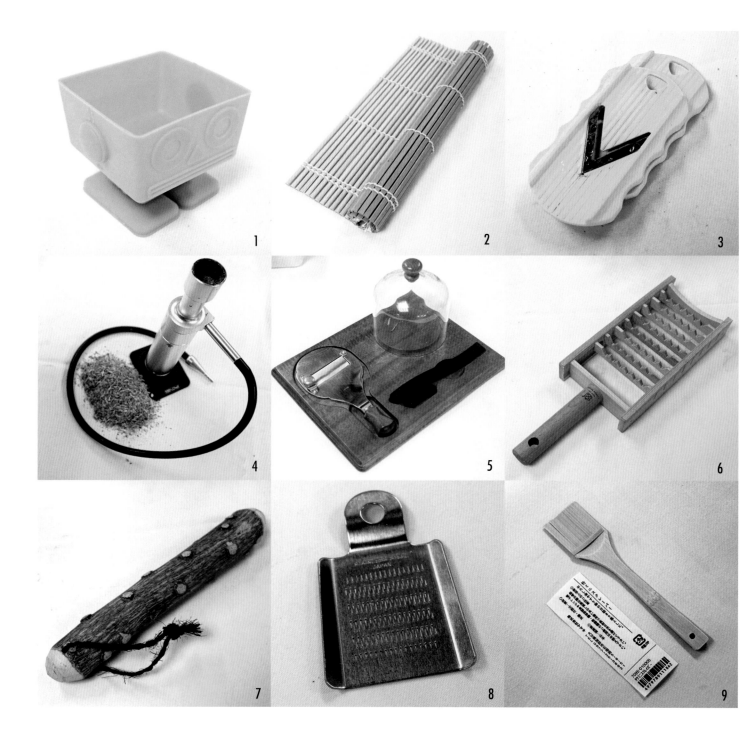

QUIPMENT

10

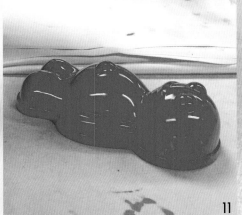

11

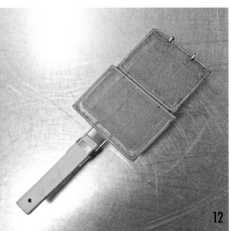

12

13

1. Oto silicone mould – Forbidden Planet
www.forbiddenplanet.com

2. Sushi mat – Harumi Kurihara shop
www.yutori.co.jp/en/shop

3. Vegetable mandolins – John Lewis Online
www.johnlewis.com

4. Smoker – Culinary Concepts
www.culinaryconcepts.co.uk

5. Truffle shaver– G. Lorenzi
www.lorenzi.it

6. Vegetable grater – Harumi Kurihara shop
www.yutori.co.jp/en/shop

7. Pestle – Harumi Kurihara shop
www.yutori.co.jp/en/shop

8. Ginger grater – Harumi Kurihara shop
www.yutori.co.jp/en/shop

9. Ginger grater cleaner – Harumi Kurihara shop
www.yutori.co.jp/en/shop

10. Bamboo steamer – New Loon Moon (Gerrard St)
www.newloonmoon.com

11. Jelly silicone mould – Forbidden Planet
www.forbiddenplanet.com

12. Grain tosser – Takashimaya (Singapore)
www.takashimaya-sin.com

13. Easy gyoza – Ekitron
www.ekitron.com

(Previous spread) Pac-Man mould – Forbidden Planet
www.forbiddenplanet.com

Published by Preface Publishing 2013

10 9 8 7 6 5 4 3 2 1

First published in Great Britain in 2013 by Preface Publishing

20 Vauxhall Bridge Road, London, SW1V 2SA

An imprint of The Random House Group Limited

www.randomhouse.co.uk

www.prefacepublishing.co.uk

Addresses for companies within The Random House Group Limited
can be found at www.randomhouse.co.uk

The Random House Group Limited Reg. No. 954009

A CIP catalogue record for this book is available from the British Library

ISBN 978 1 84809 387 4

The Random House Group Limited supports The Forest Stewardship Council® (FSC®), the leading international forest certification organisation.Our books carrying the FSC label are printed on FSC® certified paper.FSC is the only forest certification scheme endorsed by the leading environmental organisations,including Greenpeace. Our paper procurement policy can be foud at www.randomhouse.co.uk/environment

Colour reproduction by XY Digital Ltd.

Printed and bound in China by C&C Offset Printing Co., Ltd.

Yogurt jar (top left):

Nutrition | per 100g

421kJ - 101kcal
3.5g
15.0g
15.0g
3.0g
~1.9g
(Trace)
(Trace)

Ingredients

FULL-FAT PASTEURISED MILK*, CANE SUGAR*, BILBERRY* (6.3%), SKIMMED MILK POWDER*, LOCUST BEAN GUM, XANTHAN GUM, NATURAL BILBERRY FLAVOUR, YOGURT CULTURES. (*FROM ORGANIC FARMING)

Allergen Information

CONTAINS MILK.

Produced in Belgium for
©2007 Whole Foods Market IP, LP
63-97 Kensington High Street
London, W8 5SE
www.wholefoodsmarket.com

Organic Certification
Skal 4236

BE
M148
EC

ECO

Skal 4236

KEEP REFRIGERATED BELOW 8°C
USE BY: SEE DATE ON LID

150g ℮

Tomato jar (top right):

Produced by Mr. Organic in Pontinia,
just south of Rome.

STORAGE: Once opened, keep me refrigerated and I'll remain totally sumptuous for 8 weeks.

INGREDIENTS: Italian Organic Sun Ripened Tomatoes. And that's all!

NUTRITIONAL INFORMATION:
Average Nutritional Values per 100g
Energy   383 kJ / 91,6 kcal
Protein   2,18 g
Carbohydrate 10,3 g
Fat   0,3 g

NET WEIGHT: 200g ℮

BEST BEFORE...SEE TOP OF JAR.

Tetra Pak carton (bottom left):

PROTECTS WHAT'S GOOD
Tetra Pak™

Nutrition Information / Ernährungsinformationen / Information nutritionnelle / Voedingswaarde / Informazioni nutrizionali / Información nutricional:

Per 100g

Energy/Energie/Energie/Energie/Energia/Energia | 259kJ/62kcal
Protein/Eiweiß/Protéines/Proteine/Proteine/Proteínas | 7g
Carbohydrate/Kohlenhydrate/Glucides/Koolhydraten/Carboidrati/Carbohidratos | 2g
Fat/Fett/Lipides/Vet/Grassi/Grasas | 3g

(GB) Keep in a cool dry place. Refrigerate unused portions in an airtight container and use within 2 days. DO NOT FREEZE OR MICROWAVE IN PACKAGE. Best Before End: See side of pack. (D) Kühl und trocken lagern. Nach dem Öffnen in einem luftdichten Behälter gekühlt aufbewahren und innerhalb von zwei Tagen verbrauchen. NICHT EINFRIEREN ODER IN DER VERPACKUNG IN DIE MIKROWELLE GEBEN. Mindestens haltbar bis: Ende, siehe Verpackungsseite. (F) Conserver dans un endroit frais et sec. Après ouverture, placer au réfrigérateur dans un récipient hermétique et consommer dans les deux jours. NE PAS CONGELER. NE PAS PASSER AU MICRO-ONDES DANS L'EMBALLAGE. A consommer avant fin : voir sur le côté du paquet. (NL) Koel en droog bewaren. Ongeopende porties in een luchtdichte verpakking in de koelkast bewaren en binnen twee dagen gebruiken. NIET IN DE VERPAKKING BEVRIEZEN OF IN DE MAGNETRON OPWARMEN. Ten minste houdbaar tot einde: zie zijkant verpakking. (I) Conservare in un luogo asciutto. Una volta aperto, conservare in frigorifero in un recipiente chiuso e consumare entro 2 giorni. NON CONGELARE NE CUCINARE IN UN FORNO A MICROONDE SENZA AVERE PRIMA RIMOSSO LA CONFEZIONE. Da consumarsi entro: vedere lato della confezione. (E) Conservar en un lugar fresco y seco. Una vez abierto, guarde el producto en un contenedor hermético y manténgalo refrigerado. Deberá consumirlo en un máximo de 2 días. NO CONGELAR NI CALENTAR EN EL MICROONDAS SIN ANTES RETIRAR EL ENVOLTORIO. Fecha de caducidad: ver lateral del paquete.

Heinz Beanz can (bottom right):

HEINZ BEANZ

ORGANIC

Baked Beans Packed Full of The Finest Organically Grown Ingredients

SOIL ASSOCIATION ORGANIC STANDARD
ORGANIC CERTIFICATION: UK5

COOKING INSTRUCTIONS

STORAGE

DIETARY INFORMATION

NUTRITION INFORMATION

Typical Values	Per 100g	Per ½ can	GDA†
Energy - kJ	338kJ	701kJ	
-kcal (Calories)	81kcal	166kcal	2000
Protein	4.8g	9.9g	45g
Carbohydrate	12.9g	26.7g	230g
(of which sugars)	(5.1g)	(10.6g)	90g
Fat	0.2g	0.4g	70g
(of which saturates)	(Trace)	(Trace)	20g
Fibre	3.8g	7.8g	24g
Sodium	0.3g	0.6g	2.4g
Salt equivalent	0.7g	1.5g	6g

†Guideline Daily Amounts for average adults

INGREDIENTS

Beans*(52%), Tomatoes*(33%), Water, Sugar*, Cornflour, Salt, Spirit Vinegar*, Spices*, Onion Powder*

*produced in accordance with organic farming standards